Getting into

Law

James Barton

15th edition

trotman | t

Getting into Law

This 15th edition published in 2024 by Trotman, an imprint of Trotman Indigo Publishing Ltd, 21d Charles Street, Bath BA1 1HX.

© Trotman Indigo Publishing Ltd 2024

Author: James Barton

12th–14th edns: Emily Lucas
11th edn: Steven Boyes and Melanie Allen

British Library Cataloguing in Publication Data
A catalogue record for this book is available from the British Library.

ISBN 978 1 911724 02 5

All rights reserved. This book is sold subject to the condition that it shall not, by way of trade or otherwise, be lent, resold, hired out or otherwise circulated without the publisher's prior written consent in any form of binding or cover other than that in which it is published and without a similar condition including this condition being imposed on the subsequent purchaser. No part of this publication may be reproduced, stored in a retrieval system or transmitted in any form or by any means, electronic and mechanical, photocopying, recording or otherwise without prior permission of Trotman Indigo Publishing.

Every effort has been made to trace copyright holders and to obtain their permission for use of copyright material. The publisher apologises for any errors or omissions and would be grateful to be notified of any corrections that should be incorporated in future editions of this book.

Printed and bound by 4Edge Ltd, Hockley, Essex

All details in this book were correct at the time of going to press. To keep up to date with all the latest news and updates and to access the online resources that accompany this book, use this QR code or visit **trotman.co.uk/pages/getting-into-online-resources**.

Contents

	Preface	v
	About the author	v
	Acknowledgements	vi
	About this book	1
1|	**Legal eagle: An introduction to the legal profession**	**3**
	Solicitors	4
	Barristers	5
	Legal executives	5
	Other lawyers	7
	Size and make-up of the legal profession (England and Wales)	8
	Do I need a law degree?	10
	What if I don't want to go into the law after my degree?	11
2|	**Red tape: The UK's legal systems**	**14**
	The English legal system	14
	The Scottish legal system	27
	The Northern Irish legal system	28
3|	**A law unto themselves: What do lawyers do?**	**30**
	Solicitors	30
	Barristers	40
	Legal executives, paralegals and legal secretaries	44
	The legal profession in Scotland	46
	The legal profession in Northern Ireland	48
4|	**Above board: How to qualify as a lawyer**	**49**
	Solicitors: England and Wales	49
	Solicitors: Scotland	69
	Solicitors: Northern Ireland	72
	Barristers: England and Wales	76
	Advocates: Scotland	81
	Barristers: Northern Ireland	82
5|	**Due process: Getting work experience**	**83**
	What can you gain from work experience?	83
	Things to consider during work experience	85
	Where to apply for work experience	87
	How to apply	92

Contents

6|	**Conveyancing: Choosing your law degree**	**98**
	Things to consider	98
	Types of law degree	99
	Academic requirements	101
	Choosing a university	102
7|	**Fine print: The UCAS application and the LNAT**	**108**
	Suggested application timescale	108
	The UCAS form	112
	Your personal statement	113
	The reference	124
	The LNAT	125
8|	**Burden of proof: Succeeding at interview**	**128**
	What to expect at the interview	129
	Preparation for a law interview	129
	On the day: practicalities and general advice	139
	The interview for work experience	141
	Sample interview questions on legal issues	141
9|	**Letter of the law: Non-standard applications**	**143**
	Graduates with degrees other than law	143
	Mature students	143
	Overseas students	144
10|	**Open-and-shut case: Results Day**	**148**
	What to do if your grades are significantly better than anticipated	148
	What to do if you hold an offer but miss the grades	149
	What to do if you have no offer	150
	Retaking your A levels	150
	Extenuating circumstances	151
	Students with disabilities and special educational needs	153
11|	**Bail out: Fees and funding**	**155**
	UK students	155
	EU students	156
	Living expenses	156
	Funding your studies	157
	Bursaries and scholarships	159
12|	**All rights reserved: Further information**	**162**
	Useful websites	162
	Useful books	165
	Professional journals	166
	Glossary	**167**

Preface

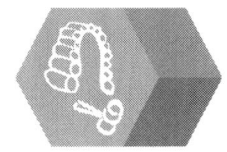

Law has always been a sought-after profession for students, and now, perhaps more than ever before, aspiring lawyers face tough competition at virtually every stage of their route to qualification, from securing a place on one of the 'best' university law degree courses to finding a job at the end of it all.

During the course of MPW's work advising students on their choice of university course and subsequent career path, we have gathered together a huge amount of information on law courses and the legal profession. With the encouragement of Trotman Indigo Publishing, that information has been brought together in this guide.

This edition has been substantially revised and updated. We hope that this guide will be useful to anyone considering a career in law.

About the author

James Barton is the Global Director of MPW Group. He read Ancient History and Classical Civilisation at the University of Warwick before undertaking an MA in Performance Philosophy. Having worked in the education sector for over 15 years, and having previously penned 22 different Trotman publications, James is well versed on the intricacies of university applications and the need to be specific in an overcrowded field. He is now a member of the MPW board and, as an Ambassador for UK education, is a sought-after international speaker on a variety of topics, specifically related to further and higher education.

Acknowledgements

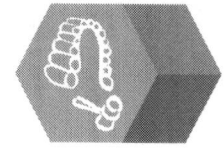

I would like to thank MPW and Trotman Education for giving me the opportunity to produce this edition of *Getting into Law*. Many thanks are due to all those who have written previous editions, in particular Emily Lucas.

My first thank you, though, should be to Joely Neilan, without whose exceptional work and research skills, this book would have taken a lot longer.

I would like to thank all of the individuals who have contributed to this book and previous editions, especially John, Daniel, Jinder, Reanna, Edward, Sam, Martin, Nina, Jessica, Henry, Stewart, Andrew, Robert, Julia, Cameron, Jade, Alesha, Alex, Emily and Sarah for their insights into applying to law courses, as well as studying and working in the field of law. I am extremely grateful that these individuals were willing to take time out of their busy schedules to contribute.

I would like to thank Alina Kononenko, for her unwavering support and commitment to education – she is a true advocate for the sector.

I would like to thank those at the Law Society, the Solicitors Regulation Authority, the Bar Council of England and Wales and the Bar Standards Board, as well as the university admissions departments, law firms and barristers' chambers who have responded to my endless pestering regarding statistics and advice.

Finally, I would like to encourage all those thinking of applying to university to do so with optimism and enthusiasm. University is a choice, and those attending should feel lucky to do so; therefore, treat the application with the respect it deserves and try your hardest. Anything is possible if you follow the advice that is given.

This book is dedicated to the memory of Gemma Barton.

About this book

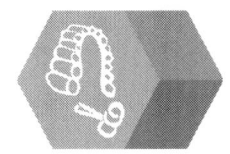

Are you the X (formerly Twitter) superstar 'The Secret Barrister'? Chances are strong that the answer to that is no. Chances are equally strong that you have not been deterred by the narrative about the conduct of some in the legal profession that raises more than a few eyebrows, as why else would you be picking up this book.

This book is written for anyone considering a career in law. Law is a perennial favourite as a career choice: it offers intellectual stimulation, ancient customs, a morally satisfying focus on justice and fairness, and potentially great financial rewards.

However, with popularity comes competition: now, more than ever before, competition for places to read law at university, for solicitors' training contract places and barristers' pupillages is intense. You will therefore need to do your research and be as fully prepared as possible. I hope that this book will go some way towards arming you with the necessary information to help you to succeed.

I once heard a King's Counsel (KC) describe the legal profession as 'gavels and giggles' – a profession for those with a quick wit and a sharp mind. I think that captures some of the legal profession perfectly. However, don't lose sight of the fact that a lot of law is simply conveyancing, which is much less fast-paced.

The book will start with an introduction to the legal profession, an overview of the UK's legal systems, and a discussion of what lawyers do.

The next two chapters will then outline how to qualify as a lawyer, including the different qualification routes, and then consider the importance of work experience.

The remaining chapters will guide you through the university application process, including choosing the right university law (or other) course, completing the UCAS form (including the all-important personal statement), preparing for an interview if necessary and what to do on results day. There is then a chapter outlining the arrangements for fees and funding for university degree courses.

At the end of the book there is a glossary of terms, relating to the study of law, applying to university and qualifying as a lawyer.

Of course, you will have to show lots of ability and drive to impress university law admissions tutors and your potential future employers. You should make sure that you:

- revise thoroughly for your exams and get the best grades you possibly can, giving you the widest choice of degree options
- become a legal eagle and do your own research. Talk to your teachers, family, friends, lawyers and anyone else who knows something about the legal profession. Consider carefully what type of degree course is appropriate for you, or, indeed, whether you should even study law and become a lawyer in the first place. There is also a huge amount of information and guidance online, which the references in this book will help you find, so make sure that you use it!

1 | Legal eagle: An introduction to the legal profession

> **Her Majesty Queen Elizabeth II**
>
> Probably the biggest change since the last edition of this book, is that Her Majesty Queen Elizabeth II passed away in September 2022. This had a significant impact on many areas of life, but specifically in the legal profession. Most notably, QCs (Queen's Counsel) were automatically renamed KCs (King's Counsel), an elite rank for barristers in the UK.

Most people's first impressions of the legal profession come from the glamorous world of film and television – think *Suits*, America's number one legal show (subjective). Legal dramas paint a picture of lawyers striding heroically across the courtroom, standing up for truth and justice. But what are lawyers and what do they actually do?

The term 'lawyer' is a loose one that covers barristers, solicitors, judges, legal executives, paralegals, in-house legal advisors, some civil servants and academic lawyers. Those whom Americans call 'lawyers' can usually be replaced with the term 'solicitor' in the UK. In England and Wales, the crucial distinction to make is between the two main branches of the profession: solicitors and barristers. The legal professions in Scotland and Northern Ireland have a similar distinction and are outlined at the end of Chapter 3. The essential difference between solicitors and barristers relates to their respective rights to advocate on behalf of a client in court: traditionally only barristers were permitted to undertake advocacy on behalf of a client in the highest courts. This distinction means that law is sometimes referred to as a 'split' profession – but the split is increasingly becoming blurred, due to modern reforms that permit solicitors to undertake further training and then represent clients in the higher courts.

> **Solicitors** work on all aspects of the law, but do not normally present their clients' cases in court.
>
> **Barristers** are instructed by solicitors to represent their clients in the courtroom or give opinions on specific points of law.

The main focus of this book is on the solicitors' and barristers' professions, but there are many other careers within the legal field that can also be pursued, and also many non-legal careers for which a law degree might provide a good foundation.

Solicitors

Solicitors are often described as being like medical general practitioners (GPs). They deal directly with their clients and often have an ongoing professional and/or business relationship with them. Solicitors in private practice group together in law firm partnerships, with the senior solicitors being partners and the more junior solicitors being employed assistants. Most solicitors now deal with specific areas of the law, for example employment or family law or, in the City, specialist areas such as syndicated loans, bonds or takeovers and mergers. In this respect they differ from GPs, who are usually generalists.

However, in most cases, law firms cover a wide area of legal practice; this means that in smaller firms solicitors may be required to cover a broader range of areas, whereas the larger law firms will have specialists in very narrow areas of law.

Historically, solicitors could only appear in lower courts, such as the magistrates' and county courts. These days, however, solicitors who obtain higher rights of audience can appear in the higher courts, including the Supreme Court, and may even apply to become KCs (King's Counsel), although this is still rare.

The Law Society is the body that represents and supports solicitors in England and Wales. The Solicitors Regulation Authority is the independent regulator of solicitors and law firms in England and Wales, and deals with all regulatory and disciplinary matters, including:

- setting the standards for qualifying as a solicitor
- administering the roll (register) of solicitors
- drafting the rules of professional conduct
- monitoring solicitors and their firms to make sure that they are complying with the rules.

Barristers

Barristers have traditionally been described as more like medical consultants. They are 'self-employed referral professionals' who are often, although not exclusively, trial lawyers – meaning that they appear robed and wigged in court on behalf of their clients. Clients are usually referred to them by a professional advisor, often a solicitor – although modern reforms allow barristers to see the public directly where the Bar Council has agreed that no referral is necessary (for example in relation to tax advice when referred by an accountant).

It is usual for barristers (often called counsel) to specialise in certain areas of law, such as criminal law, company law or tax law and so on. Barristers in private practice group together in chambers, sharing overheads and office support, but remaining self-employed professionals.

Barristers in England and Wales are represented by the Bar Council, which promotes barristers' services and upholds ethical standards in the profession. The Bar Standards Board performs a similar function to the Solicitors Regulation Authority, and is responsible for regulating barristers in the public interest. Its functions include:

- setting the education and training requirements for becoming a barrister
- setting the standards of conduct for barristers
- monitoring the service provided by barristers.

Legal executives

Legal executives are lawyers who have not undertaken the professional training required to become a solicitor or barrister, but have qualified instead with the Chartered Institute of Legal Executives (CILEX, www.cilex.org.uk). CILEX is a professional association and governing body for those training to become lawyers, legal executives, paralegals and other legal professionals.

Historically, the modern legal executive role evolved from the role of law clerks, who used to help solicitors with their cases. In the 1960s, the legal executives' profession was created in order to offer a recognised career path.

The Legal Services Act 2007 made chartered legal executives 'authorised persons' who are able to undertake 'reserved legal activities' alongside solicitors and barristers. Qualified chartered legal executives can now do much of the same work that solicitors do, but are trained to work in one or two areas of the law rather than having a broader, more general role. Typical day-to-day tasks of legal executives might include preparing contracts, advising clients on legal matters, contacting professionals on their behalf or representing them in court.

Getting into Law

From June 2021, all former CILEX training routes were replaced by the CILEX Professional Qualification (CPQ), which provides a more flexible and affordable pathway to becoming a CILEX lawyer, advanced paralegal or paralegal.

By studying the CILEX CPQ, students will cover core legal knowledge, ethics and professional responsibility, practice and skills and professional experience. The professional experience component is acquired through legal employment. There are three stages to the CPQ – Foundation, Advanced and Professional – which allow individuals to enter at a level that reflects their prior experience and qualifications, as determined by the training provider. Along with the reform to their qualifications, CILEX have also introduced new titles for their professionals: CILEX Lawyer (who will have practice rights), CILEX Paralegal and CILEX Advanced Paralegal – for those completing the Professional, Foundation and Advanced stages respectively. CILEX Lawyers have parity with solicitors as a consequence of them holding practice rights in their specialist area.

> **Further Information about the CILEX CPQ**
>
> There are a number of pathways available with the CPQ, including:
>
> - immigration
> - probate
> - family law
> - business and employment law
> - conveyancing
> - criminal law and litigation
> - dispute resolution.
>
> In total, there are 22 modules across the CPQ.
>
> - The CPQ Foundation stage comprises five mandatory modules.
> - The CPQ Advanced stage comprises four mandatory modules and one optional module (from a selection of three).
> - The CPQ Professional stage comprises one mandatory module and one optional module (from a selection of nine).
>
> Trainees who wish to practise in dispute resolution, family litigation or criminal litigation will also need to take CILEX's advocacy course.

Other lawyers

The Legal Services Act 2007 also defined various other groups of lawyers as being entitled to undertake reserved legal activities. These lawyers are trained and qualified in particular specialist areas of law and often work in law firms alongside solicitors. They are notaries (www.thenotariessociety.org.uk), licensed conveyancers (www.clc-uk.org), law costs draftsmen (www.associationofcostslawyers.co.uk), trademark attorneys (www.itma.org.uk) and patent attorneys (www.cipa.org.uk).

Case study

Prior to becoming a patent attorney, John had his sights set on becoming a research scientist. It was while studying for his biochemistry degree at the University of Oxford that he had his eyes opened to the prospect of a career in law instead.

'Throughout my biochemistry degree, I had always assumed that I would want to work in research after graduation. The intellectual stimulation that research presents was always appealing to me. However, during my fourth year, I undertook a research project in the field of pharmacology and stumbled across patents in action. I was intrigued by the legal processes involved in patenting and contacted some UK companies to undertake work experience in that field. After a few short weeks, I decided this was the career path that I wanted to embark on.

'Following graduation, I commenced a role as a patent attorney in training in the field of life sciences. After four years of working in the role, I successfully completed all of my qualifying Patent Examination Board and European Patent Office examinations and, as such, qualified as a UK and European patent attorney. I opted to move to the Munich branch of the company that I was working for to work in their life sciences department.

'The work that I do ranges from supporting companies with employee inventions, advising on product marketing in the field of health care, regulatory issues with clinical trials, production and distribution, and licence agreements for research and development cooperations. A typical day might involve meeting with clients and advising whether something is patentable, filing applications and advising on how to use a patent. On occasion, I might also need to defend a client in a patent challenge, or challenge patents that infringe upon those of my clients.'

Size and make-up of the legal profession (England and Wales)

Solicitors

The solicitors' profession in England and Wales is the largest branch of the legal profession. In July 2021, the Law Society (www.lawsociety.org.uk), which acts as the governing body for solicitors, reported that there were 209,215 registered solicitors, and 153,282 of these held a practising certificate – the highest total recorded to date. The numbers have been steadily growing over the past decade, and are forecast to continue at a similar rate.

The solicitors' profession is divided between solicitors who work in private practice for law firms and those who work 'in-house' (i.e. for companies, government legal departments and so on). In 2021, private law firms employed 97,414 solicitors with practising certificates, while those working in-house amounted to 55,868.

In 2021, of all the practising solicitors, 80,870 were women, making up more than 52% of that cohort. The proportion of practising solicitors who are from minority ethnic backgrounds was 14.8% in 2021.

The Covid-19 pandemic, which marked 2020, had notable effects on the profession, resulting in an 11% decrease in trainee registrations. Interestingly, the City of London hosted a third of all trainees, despite the challenges posed by the pandemic. However, the number of graduates earning law degrees from universities in England and Wales continued to rise, exceeding 17,000 in 2020.

In terms of geographical distribution, Greater London was home to a substantial portion of the legal profession in 2021, hosting 42% of all solicitors in England and Wales.

Barristers

The barristers' profession, known as the Bar, is much smaller than the solicitors' profession. Barristers with practising certificates may work as self-employed barristers, employed barristers, or as dual practitioners, with the majority being self-employed. Self-employed barristers work in chambers or as sole practitioners. Some barristers practise in a dual capacity, undertaking both employed and self-employed work

According to the Bar Standards Board (www.barstandardsboard.org.uk), there were a total of 17,538 barristers in practice in 2022, of whom 38% were women and 15% described themselves as belonging to an ethnic minority. Most practising barristers (13,926 in 2022) are self-employed; a further 3,120 are in employed practice.

1 An introduction to the legal profession

	Number	% women (approx)	% in London (approx)
Solicitors	152,282	52.1%	41.3%
– private practice	– 97,414		
– in-house	– 55,868		
Barristers	17,538	38%	64%
– self-employed	– 13,926		
– employed	– 3,120		
– dual capacity	– 492		

Table 1: Solicitors and barristers in practice (England and Wales), most recent statistics available

Legal executives and other lawyers

The much younger profession of legal executives is smaller still: the Chartered Institute of Legal Executives (www.cilex.org.uk) reported in 2023 that there were 8,191 qualified chartered legal executives, of whom more than a thousand were partners in law firms. The total number of members of the Institute (including paralegals and other legal professionals) was around 21,000, of whom 77% were women. More than a third of their new members are of an ethnic minority.

The other groups of lawyers mentioned above (notaries, licensed conveyancers, law costs draftsmen, trademark attorneys and patent attorneys) are also much smaller in number than solicitors or barristers. This book will therefore focus on the two main branches of the legal profession: solicitors and barristers.

Gender balance

It is difficult to imagine that less than 100 years ago the legal profession was the preserve of men. Things have changed and are still changing. The Law Society reports that just over 60% of training contracts were issued to women in 2021. Some 52% of practising solicitors are female, and, in July 2021, there were nearly 8,930 female partners in law firms. Around 60% of practising solicitors under the age of 35 are now women. The Law Society's most recent report suggests that the number of women practising as solicitors exceeds the number of men working in the profession, and this has been the case for a number of years.

There has been a feeling within the solicitors' profession in the past that not enough female solicitors make it to partnership in some of the very large law firms, and there is still a substantial difference between the representation of men and women at partner level, with women currently representing 34% of partners. In larger firms with more than 50 partners, there is an even smaller percentage of female partners: 27%, with a 35% representation in smaller firms (typically two to five partners). However, the gap has been narrowing over recent years. The percentage of women solicitors working outside private practice, i.e. in-house, is higher.

Some 38% of practising barristers are women, with 39% of new entrants undertaking pupillage being female. Whereas in the past it was difficult for women to break down the traditional barriers, today the profession is increasingly open to all. This is evident in the fact that in 2021–2 just over 54.2% of barristers called to the Bar were women.

However, there is still progress to be made by women in terms of judicial appointments. In 2021 only 34% of court judges were female, though there was greater representation among tribunal judges, of which 50% were women. Over the last few years, the number of women in these roles has increased, but this trend has not been reflected in senior court appointments; only 29% of judges in the High Court and above are women. Only three women have made it to the most senior judicial appointment of the Supreme Court; in 2017, Lady Hale became the first female president of the Supreme Court since its creation. Lady Hale was open in her criticism of the lack of female representation in the Supreme Court and about the importance of diversity in a body that must make decisions that represent society. Following the retirement of Lady Hale and Lady Black, Lady Justice Rose was appointed as a second female justice in the UK's highest court. However, significant concerns remain around the lack of diversity in the all-white panel. Efforts are being made to increase the number of female judges and the number is increasing every year. It will, however, take time before parity can be reached.

Do I need a law degree?

The legal profession in England and Wales is virtually unique in not requiring all entrants to have a law degree. In fact, many non-law graduates enter the profession through the full-time Graduate Diploma in Law programme, which is an intensive one-year postgraduate course for non-law graduates covering the essential foundation subjects taught as part of a law degree. A substantial percentage of non-law graduates are direct entrants into the solicitors' profession, and many UK-domiciled students enrolled on the Bar Professional Training Course (BPTC) have a non-law related undergraduate background. This demonstrates that the skills acquired on many non-law degrees are often highly sought after by legal recruiters. For example, language skills or scientific/technical skills may be particularly useful in certain areas of law, and humanities degrees teach and test many of the skills that are essential for a lawyer, such as the ability to research information and analyse and present it in a clear and concise way. It is therefore important to bear in mind that you do not need a law degree to become a lawyer and many employers positively welcome applications from non-law graduates who can offer broader skills in other areas. There are, however, cost implications due to the extra year of postgraduate study that will be required (see Chapter 4, page 54 for more details).

It is also important to be aware that not every law degree is recognised by the professional bodies as a qualifying law degree (QLD) that will satisfy the requirements for the academic stage of training. It depends on the subjects that are studied on the course. This means that, if you do decide to do a law degree, you must be careful when choosing your course. The Solicitors Regulation Authority (SRA) and the Bar Standards Board (BSB) keep registers of which degrees are approved QLDs and these are available on their respective websites. They are also discussed further in Chapter 6.

What if I don't want to go into the law after my degree?

As well as those who, unfortunately, do not manage to get into one of the legal professions after taking a law degree, there are some students who study law with no intention of becoming a professional lawyer. The legal knowledge and additional skills gained from a law degree are highly prized and can be applied to a number of jobs.

But what else can a law graduate do other than law? Many public figures have degrees in law that have led them in all sorts of different directions, from politicians to comedians. Some of the careers that a law degree can lead to are listed below.

- **Accountancy.** Many aspects of accountancy relate to those found in legal practice, such as analysing large amounts of technical material, writing reports and advising clients. Law graduates are often particularly attracted by tax consultancy.
- **Civil service.** If you are interested in policy making and implementation, then you might think about a career in the civil service. Administrators such as civil servants need a methodical and precise approach, as well as good writing and communication skills – all skills that are developed and honed on a law degree course. Some government departments, such as the Home Office, HM Revenue & Customs, the Ministry of Justice and the Foreign, Commonwealth and Development Office, have particular legal responsibilities and might be especially attractive to law graduates. Local government and the health services are also possibilities for public sector careers in administration.
- **Commerce and industry.** The skills you learn from a law degree will also be invaluable in the world of commerce and industry, where there are career opportunities in general business management.

Getting into Law

- **Banking and finance.** A number of law graduates are lured into the highly paid world of banking and finance, where a legal background can certainly be useful.

Law graduates also go into many other areas, such as legal publishing, the media, journalism (legal or otherwise), the police service, teaching, human resources and more.

Some law graduates choose not to pursue the training to become either a solicitor or a barrister, or, indeed a legal executive, but would still like to do something in the legal field. They will often move into areas such as paralegal or clerking work. Paralegals research cases, scan and collate documents and generally assist qualified lawyers in their work. Clerks undertake duties such as taking witness statements on behalf of solicitors' clients and conducting legal research for solicitors, barristers and others plus any administrative work that is required.

> **Case study**
>
> Dan completed his undergraduate degree in law at the University of Warwick, and used the skillset that he had acquired to pursue a career in accountancy.
>
> 'I was always drawn towards the study of law because of the academic challenges that it presented. I thought I wanted to pursue a career in the field, ideally as a barrister, but while I enjoyed the study of law, it wasn't something I could see myself doing for the rest of my life. This was confirmed for me when I undertook work experience during the course of my undergraduate study.
>
> 'After graduating, I knew I would miss the challenge of academic study and so I decided to pursue a role in an accounting firm. I worked as an accounts payable clerk for several years, which allowed me to get to grips with what the field of accounting was like. In this role, I mainly undertook clerical tasks, such as processing invoices and tracking payments. After deciding I wanted to work in accounting, I started studying for the ACCA exams and qualified over a period of four years, during which time I worked in a number of slightly different roles with varying companies, including junior accountant and assistant accountant. After qualifying, I took on a management accountant role which allowed me to work towards my current position as a finance manager. In this role, I work with companies on financial planning, financial analysis and looking into finance operations.
>
> 'I was able to pursue a career in accounting because of the strong skillset that I developed through studying law, which is a very

challenging subject that stretches you intellectually and instils resilience. Law also allows you to get a better understanding of broader industry sectors. In the interview process, I was able to draw on my experiences in working with law firms – having an understanding of how different sectors overlap. As an accountant, my law degree has given me a better understanding of how the law influences accounting practices. Having a law degree from a good university is viewed as a strong platform for graduate positions, and I think this helped enormously in getting me to where I am now.'

Did you hear about the man who sued an airline company after it mislaid his luggage? Sadly, he lost his case.

2 | Red tape: The UK's legal systems

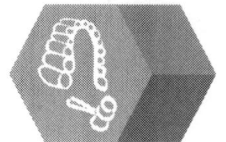

This chapter looks predominantly at the legal system in England and Wales, with the Scottish and Northern Irish legal systems briefly outlined at the end of the chapter. Welsh and English law are really one and the same, with a few important differences, such as the Wales-only laws passed (pertaining to devolved matters only) by the Senedd. And the Welsh Language Act 1993 puts the Welsh language on an equal footing with English in the conduct of public business and the administration of justice in Wales. See https://senedd.wales for more information.

The English legal system

English law comes from two main sources: statute law made by Parliament (also known as 'Acts of Parliament' or 'legislation') and case law made by judges (also known as 'common law'). The UK's membership of the European Union significantly impacted on the English legal system historically, and following the execution of Brexit in January 2020, changes are now underway on the system again. These changes are summarised below, followed by a description of the court structure.

- End of the supremacy of EU Law: With the UK's departure from the EU, the principle of the supremacy of EU law over UK law no longer applied. This meant that UK courts were no longer bound to follow decisions of the European Court of Justice (ECJ) and could make their own interpretations of UK law.
- Incorporation of EU Law into UK law: To ensure legal continuity and clarity, the UK government passed the European Union (Withdrawal) Act 2018. This act incorporated existing EU law into UK law, creating a body of retained EU law. The UK Supreme Court became the highest authority for interpreting and applying this retained EU law.
- Changes in jurisdiction and enforcement: The UK no longer participates in the EU's legal framework, which includes the European Arrest Warrant and certain aspects of civil judicial cooperation. This has led to changes in the way the UK handles issues such as extradition and cross-border legal disputes.

- Trade agreements: The UK has negotiated and signed various trade agreements with other countries, including a trade agreement with the EU known as the EU-UK Trade and Cooperation Agreement. These agreements can have legal implications in various areas, including trade, competition law and intellectual property.
- Regulatory divergence: One of the potential consequences of Brexit was that the UK could adopt different regulations and standards from the EU in areas such as product safety, environmental law and data protection. This could affect businesses operating in both the UK and the EU.
- Immigration and citizenship: The UK introduced a points-based immigration system, ending the free movement of EU citizens to the UK. There were changes to the rights and status of EU citizens living in the UK and UK citizens living in the EU.
- Dispute resolution: The EU-UK Trade and Cooperation Agreement established a dispute resolution mechanism to address disputes arising from the agreement. This included the possibility of arbitration and the imposition of tariffs or trade restrictions in certain cases.

Statute law

Parliament is the supreme law-making body in the English legal system, and is made up of the House of Commons and the House of Lords. The House of Commons is made up of 650 democratically elected Members of Parliament (MPs) from various political parties, and it is the political party that has the majority of MPs elected to the House of Commons that will form a government. It is worth noting that in 2017, there was a two-thirds vote for a snap election. Despite winning a majority in 2015, the Conservative Party failed to do so in 2017, so entered into an informal coalition with the Democratic Unionist Party (DUP), whereby the DUP aimed to support governmental bills and display confidence in the government. In 2019 the government's ability to maintain a majority in Parliament became even more precarious, with MPs defecting (formally changing the political party they represent in the Commons) and losing the party whip (having their status as an MP for a given party revoked) over Brexit and Boris Johnson's suspension of Parliament. The smaller the majority a government has, the harder it can be for them to pass laws. However, in December 2019 another snap election was held in an attempt to break the deadlock on Brexit. This time, Johnson's Conservative party won with a considerable majority of 365 seats, thus strengthening their ability to pass laws.

The House of Lords is made up of the most senior bishops in the Church of England and life peers who are nominated by the Prime Minister and then appointed by the Monarch. There are also currently 92 hereditary peers (people who have inherited their seats in the Lords) – these are eventually being phased out due to concerns about their appointment being unmeritocratic. Since the 1990s, there have been calls for reform of the House of Lords, including the suggestion that a proportion of the members be democratically elected. In May 2011, the government published detailed proposals for reform of the House of Lords, but the plans were dropped in August 2012. Instead, the House of Lords Reform Act 2014 introduced much more minor reforms, including allowing Lords to retire or be disqualified for non-attendance. In 2017, Baron Lloyd Webber retired from the House of Lords, which is something he would have been unable to do prior to these reforms. Since then, 171 peers have resigned or retired, and eight have had their rights revoked due to the Act. Despite these changes, the Lords as a body is often criticised, largely due to the fact that the individuals are unelected and to the phenomenon of silent peers: an estimated 300 Lords have never spoken in a debate since their appointment.

In addition to concerns about how politically inactive some peers are, there are criticisms about the appointments system which can be subject to misuse. Take, as a prime example, the resignation list of former Prime Minister, Boris Johnson. Over 15 years after the Cash for Honours scandal highlighted deficiencies in the award of life peerages, Johnson brought into focus another pre-existing flaw in the system: the use of the peerage allocations as personal rewards to those loyal to the outgoing leader. Johnson's list was deeply controversial and mismanaged, elevating those to the Upper House who had no reason to be there, triggering by-elections in the House of Commons, and even trying to raise the status of his own father, a man who had been subject to claims of perpetrating domestic abuse.

A report published in October 2017 by the then speaker of the Lords, Norman Fowler, stated that in order to maintain confidence in the Chamber, it should be reduced in size to no more than 600 members, with new peers being limited to 15-year terms. While the majority of appointed members are able to make valuable and significant contributions, many know very little about what the role can entail. Introducing an element of screening to the process would prevent any new influx from 'diluting' the quality of the Lords.

Despite concerns about its composition and unelected status, the Lords can provide a useful democratic function in that they are able to effectively scrutinise government and parliamentary decisions without fear of electoral recriminations; this can make them bolder. In some instances, the Lords have used their position to defeat controversial government bills or amend them to ensure human rights are protected. This can be seen by the Dubs amendment to the Immigration Bill (2016) which forced the government to arrange the relocation of a determined number of child refugees that come to the UK.

At the time of writing, in 2023, there were 785 peers in the House of Lords. Only the Chinese National People's Congress is a bigger chamber. Sir Keir Starmer, the leader of the opposition, has – if the

Labour Party were to be elected into government – promised reform within five years of taking power. Starmer has labelled the House of Lords undemocratic and wishes to revert to former Prime Minister Gordon Brown's earlier plans of an Assembly of Nations and Regions. This would be for roughly 200 members. However, the selection process is still without thought and full of problems – not least that it would create gridlock in policy making, there would be a loss of the inexpertise of those who have sat in the chamber for a long time and it would undermine the House of Commons. There is a reason why reform of the House of Lords is a perennial debate.

What else have the Lords changed?

- Ensured that protections were in place for low-paid workers before cuts to tax credits were actioned.
- Put in place safeguards for vulnerable people, including pregnant women, in immigration detention.
- Banned smoking in vehicles carrying children.
- Introduced a client money protection scheme for property agents to protect the money of landlords and tenants.
- Ensured that children with special educational needs are given the same legal support in academies as in other mainstream schools.

At interview, you might be asked to comment on proposed House of Lords reforms, such as those mentioned above, and discuss the role of this unelected chamber within a parliamentary democracy. See Chapter 8 for further considerations for interview preparations.

New laws are mostly put forward by the government, and these are known as public bills. However, not all bills come from government – backbencher MPs and opposition parties can propose private member bills, which have the potential to be transformative. Both the fox hunting ban and the smoking ban originated from private members' bills.

Following its proposal to Parliament, draft legislation has to go through several stages of debates and votes in both the House of Commons and the House of Lords prior to its passage. In the vast majority of cases, the draft legislation has to be approved by both Houses in order for it to become law. On occasion, bills are passed back and forth between the Houses in a process known as 'parliamentary ping pong' – the Investigatory Powers Act (2016) went back and forth four times prior to its passage. The final stage in the legislative process is Royal Assent, which is where the Monarch gives approval to the draft legislation and at this point it becomes an Act of Parliament. This is merely a formality and the last time that a monarch refused assent was in 1707.

Typically, Acts of Parliament cannot be challenged by the courts, and can only be changed by a subsequent piece of legislation. Acts of Parliament are also known as 'primary legislation' because they are made by

Parliament, the supreme law-making body. Parliament can delegate its law-making power to other bodies, including government departments and local authorities, and law made by such bodies is known as delegated legislation or secondary legislation. Delegated legislation is subject to the control of Parliament and can be challenged in the courts.

Common law

Although Parliament is the supreme law-making body, and judges are simply supposed to apply the laws made by Parliament in cases, the doctrine of judicial precedent and the rules of statutory interpretation mean that in practice judges also make law through decided cases. This is known as 'case law' or 'common law' and is a major source of law in the English legal system.

The doctrine of judicial precedent is based on the Latin maxim 'stare decisis' which means 'stand by what has been decided', so, very simply, when a judge makes a decision in a case, this should be followed in future cases that are similar. The system of precedent operates through the court hierarchy, so that only certain (higher) courts create binding precedents (precedents that must be followed in future cases). Precedents are created when a new situation or point of law comes up in a case that is not provided for in legislation and has not been decided in a previous case, so the judge has to decide the case by looking at situations that are similar and use reasoning by analogy.

When judges are applying legislation to cases before them, it is not always possible to simply take the words of the statute and decide the case, because words can have more than one meaning. In addition, new technology and changes in society can mean that it is not clear whether the legislation applies in some cases. This is where the rules of statutory interpretation come in. Some judges take a 'literal approach' of applying the ordinary meaning of the words in the legislation even if this leads to an absurd result, whereas other judges take a 'purposive approach' and decide the case based on what they think Parliament wanted to achieve through the legislation. When a judge makes an interpretation in a case, this can create a precedent so that future cases must follow this interpretation.

Cases to consider

In the USA, the Supreme Court (comprising the nine most senior judges and appointed by the President) uses the Constitution to determine the outcomes of cases. There are two strands of judicial outlook – strict constructionist (originalist) and loose constructionist (right to privacy).

> In its ruling, **Roe v. Wade (1973)** led to the legalisation of nationwide abortion in the United States and is viewed as a seminal ruling. It has since been used to keep abortion legal, despite the plethora of pro-life groups and pro-life politicians in existence in the United States. However, this case also raises questions surrounding the Supreme Court's power – some believe that this ruling involved the judges going beyond their jurisdiction and that the US Supreme Court justices should simply guard the constitution.
>
> This is one of the most controversial cases in the USA, with Roe v. Wade (1973) being overturned in 2022. The state of Mississippi argued that *stare decisis* ('to stand by things decided') was weak in this case because it dealt with constitutional interpretation and was controversial from the outset, therefore could not be effectively used as established law. Without it, 13 states with 'trigger laws' immediately banned abortion with the overturning of Roe.
>
> Other cases related to reproductive rights that you might choose to read include:
>
> - Planned Parenthood v. Casey (overturned at the request of the state of Mississippi along with Roe v. Wade)
> - Gonzales v. Carhart.

Common law as a source of law only works because of the system of law reporting in England and Wales; an accurate record of decided cases is kept so that it can be referred to by judges and lawyers in future cases. It is mostly decisions of the higher courts in the English legal system that are reported, and all High Court, Court of Appeal and Supreme Court cases are now available on the internet, for example from the British and Irish Legal Information Institute (www.bailii.org).

European Union law

Following the UK joining the European Economic Community (EEC) in 1973, its legal system became closely aligned with the European Union (EU) and many of the legislative and legal changes that happened in the UK in the years that followed had links to EU law. Despite the fact that Brexit has weakened the ties between UK and European law, a knowledge of European Union law is still required of UK lawyers, especially given that some elements of European law have been retained post-Brexit.

The EEC was established in 1957 by Germany, France, Italy, Belgium, the Netherlands and Luxembourg. In 1993, the EEC became the EU. Over the years European law has had an increasing impact on the legal systems of member states. There are now 27 member states.

The European Union produces its own primary and secondary legislation, and has its own court, the European Court of Justice. Case law has confirmed that European law is supreme over the national laws of member states, and that national law must be interpreted in accordance with European law. The principle of supremacy of EU law no longer applies to any UK laws made or passed after 31 January 2020, meaning that, in theory, national laws that contradict EU law could be introduced. This is, however, unlikely to happen. While the UK can no longer take cases to the European Court of Justice, it is unlikely that we will be entirely beyond their reach, as trading with the EU means that the UK will have to comply with EU standards, which are governed by the European Court of Justice.

Following Brexit, the 'Retained EU law' came into effect following the European Union (Withdrawal) Act 2018. This act took a 'snapshot' of EU law as it applied to the UK and laid the framework for it to be applied into UK law domestic law. In May 2023, the government did away with the sunset clause that intended to revoke most retained EU law at the end of 2023. The government instead have set out the revocation of 600 retained EU laws, with the remainder retained, a move that has been welcomed by The Law Society in the UK.

Cases to consider

In the **R (Factortame Ltd) v. Secretary of State for Transport (1989)** case, a group of Spanish fishermen claimed that the United Kingdom was in breach of European Union law regarding fishing boat ownership. This was the first time that the European Court of Justice restrained and overturned an Act of Parliament for contradicting European law.

So while there will be continuity in terms of some EU laws, one potential change post-Brexit may be that individuals will no longer be able to hold the UK to account for actions that are deemed contrary to the European Convention on Human Rights through appealing to the European Court of Human Rights. The highest court of appeal in the UK is the Supreme Court, but UK individuals can also take cases to the European Court of Human Rights. This is particularly useful in cases related to the UK government contravening its citizens' human rights. For instance, in a case entitled Hurst v. United Kingdom in 2005, the UK was called to account under the convention for not allowing prisoners the right to vote. The European Court of Human Rights ruled this a breach of the convention on human rights. The European Court of Justice has been something of a political hot potato, with the UK government's stance varying but ultimately stating that they are maintaining the position of ending the role of the European Court of Justice in resolving UK–EU disputes.

Human Rights Act 1998

The Human Rights Act 1998 officially incorporated the European Convention on Human Rights into the English legal system. The Convention sets out certain fundamental rights of the citizens of Europe, including the right to life, the right to a fair trial and the right to respect for private and family life. Prior to the Human Rights Act 1998, English citizens who believed that their human rights had been infringed had to take their case to the European Court of Human Rights in Strasbourg. The Human Rights Act 1998 means that such cases can be dealt with in the courts of the English legal system.

The Human Rights Act 1998 has affected the English legal system in several other ways, including the obligation for our courts to take into account any decision of the European Court of Human Rights, and, so far as it is possible to do so, interpret national legislation so that it is compatible with the European Convention on Human Rights. All draft legislation must also state whether or not it is compatible with the Convention. This is intended to encourage the government and civil service to consider the human rights implications of proposed legislation before it is introduced.

In 2015, the Conservative government proposed replacing the Human Rights Act with a British Bill of Rights. The Human Rights Act has been deemed by some to be controversial, as it has been used as a means to protect individuals such as the Muslim cleric Abu Qatada, who was accused of having links to terrorist organisations, from extradition.

Cases to consider

The **Othman (Abu Qatada) v. United Kingdom (2012)** case is an interesting case to consider in the context of human rights. Abu Qatada, a Jordanian national, required refugee status in the United Kingdom. Qatada having been convicted in absentia by Jordan on the grounds of terrorism, the United Kingdom planned to deport him. Under Article 6 of the European Convention on Human Rights, the European Court of Human Rights ruled that Qatada could not be lawfully deported owing to the risk of torture upon his return.

Qatada was ultimately deported to Jordan on the basis that he would be tried fairly by the Jordanian State Security Court and would not be subject to torture, but the case made for considerable debate.

> Other interesting cases to consider regarding the controversial elements of human rights include those associated with:
> - the killers of James Bulger (1993)
> - the Libyan soldiers convicted of sex attacks in the UK (2015).

Upon leaving the European Union, the UK was still committed to the European Convention on Human Rights. However, in December 2020, the UK Government announced its plans to review the Human Rights Act (HRA) in the UK. The Independent Human Rights Act Review set out to explore how the domestic courts and the European Court of Human Rights were working together, and the relationship between the judiciary and the legislature as a result of the impact of the Human Rights Act. Following a public call for evidence that ended in March 2021, the review panel outlined the following options for reform for the government to respond to.

- Increase knowledge and awareness
- Put the common law, UK case law and domestic legislation centre stage
- Encourage judicial dialogue
- Defuse concerns about the controversial rule of interpretation in the HRA
- Increased transparency where UK courts decide cases through the creation of an official judgements database
- Introduce a discretion to make ex-gratia payments
- Increase parliamentary scrutiny of human rights decisions by UK courts through an enhanced role for the Parliamentary Joint Committee on Human Rights
- Introduce suspended quashing orders
- Propose a national conversation and inter-governmental discussions on the extra-territorial scope of the European Convention on Human Rights and the HRA
- Amend remedial orders so that a Henry VIII power (overriding a primary legislation with a delegated legislation) cannot be used to amend the HRA itself.

Further information about the Independent Human Rights Act Review can be found at www.gov.uk/guidance/independent-human-rights-act-review.

Court structure

The court structure in England is divided into two systems: those courts with civil jurisdiction and those with criminal jurisdiction. Civil cases are private disputes between individuals or companies. There are many different types of civil law, including family law, employment law, the law of contract, the law of tort and commercial law. Criminal cases are where the state prosecutes people for breaking laws, even though there is usually a victim.

Most civil cases are heard, in the first instance, by the county courts, but in cases where large amounts of money are in dispute, they will initially be heard in the High Court. Appeals from both the county courts and the High Court can be made upwards through the court hierarchy.

All minor criminal matters are dealt with by the magistrates' court. Serious cases are referred to the crown court. Here, the case will be decided upon by a lay jury, a fundamental part of the criminal justice system. Cases can be appealed from the magistrates' court to the crown court and from there to the Court of Appeal (Criminal Division).

The highest court in the land is now the UK Supreme Court, which is the final court of appeal for civil cases throughout the UK, and for criminal cases from England, Wales and Northern Ireland. The Supreme Court replaced the Appellate Committee of the House of Lords in 2009. It only considers appeals that concern points of law of general public or constitutional importance. Each case is normally heard by five Justices of the Supreme Court.

When a court is considering a point of European law it may refer to the European Court of Justice in Luxembourg for interpretation. However, the UK government ended ties with the European Court of Justice on the completion of the withdrawal agreement (31 December 2020). Some argue that this has allowed the location of sovereignty to be returned to the UK, meaning that we have the utmost power regarding judicial decisions and that European Court of Justice rulings have no bearing on us.

The Judicial Committee of the Privy Council is the court of final appeal for many current and former Commonwealth countries, UK overseas territories and Crown dependencies. During 2021–22 the Privy Council heard 34 appeals. By far the most contentious work relates to appeals against the death penalty.

Cases to consider

The really interesting UK Supreme Court Case of **AM (Zimbabwe) (Appellant) v. Secretary of State for the Home Department (Respondent) (2019)** reflects the complexity of the cases that make their way to the Supreme Court, and is a good example when considering the rights of people who have been convicted of offences.

Getting into Law

In this case:

- The Supreme Court was asked to consider whether the return of AM to Zimbabwe would violate his right (under Article 3 of the European Convention on Human Rights) to not be subjected to inhumane treatment by reason of his medical condition (following the decision of the European Court of Human Rights in Paposhvili v. Belgium in 2017).
- AM is a national of Zimbabwe who arrived in the UK aged 13 in 2000 to join his mother.
- In 2004, AM was granted indefinite leave to remain in the UK.
- In 2006, AM was convicted for possession of a firearm and supply of heroin.
- After a sentence of nine years in jail, the Secretary of State sought to deport AM.
- However, AM is HIV-positive and is currently receiving Eviplera, an antiretroviral drug not available in Zimbabwe.
- AM appealed his deportation on medical grounds and the impact it would have on his wife and child.
- First-Tier Tribunal, Upper Tribunal and the Court of Appeal dismissed the appeal based on Article 3 and Article 8 of the European Convention on Human Rights.
- The Supreme Court unanimously allowed the appeal and remitted the case to the Upper Tribunal and, after a lengthy case, the appeal was dismissed in 2022 and AM was deported.

Judges

In contrast with many other European countries, the judiciary in England and Wales is not a separate career. Judges are appointed from both main branches of the legal profession. Chartered legal executives can also now become judges.

Judges in the Supreme Court are known as Justices of the Supreme Court (formerly Law Lords in the House of Lords) and judges in the Court of Appeal are known as Lord or Lady Justices of Appeal. In the High Court, there are High Court judges and also masters and registrars, who hear certain types of applications.

Circuit judges, recorders and district judges are the remaining three types of judges. Circuit judges sit either in the crown court (to try criminal cases) or in the county courts (to hear civil cases). Recorders are part-time circuit judges, and district judges sit in the magistrates' courts and county courts.

Alternatively, a panel of lay magistrates can try criminal cases in the magistrates' court. They are not legally qualified or paid but are respected members of the community who sit as magistrates on a part-time basis.

New members of the judiciary are selected by the Judicial Appointments Commission, an independent body that was created specifically for this purpose following the Constitutional Reform Act 2005. The aim was to provide a fair and transparent selection process. Once appointed, judges are completely independent of both the legislature and the executive, and so are free to administer justice without fear of political interference. Justices of the Supreme Court are not selected by the Judicial Appointments Commission, but are instead selected by a special Supreme Court Selection Commission.

Case study

His Honour Judge Jinder Singh Boora is a circuit judge who, unusually, works in three different courts – Leicester, Northampton and Stoke-on-Trent – on primarily weighty criminal cases.

'As a circuit judge, I sit on serious criminal cases such as terrorism, robbery, fraud and rape. I also undertake money claims involving private individuals and companies. Working in three different courts allows me to undertake a rich variety of work and meet many different people.

'My typical day involves conducting trials, in which people give evidence and juries decide whether an accused person is guilty. If an accused is found guilty or pleads guilty, I will sentence them. This is not necessarily imprisonment; I have other powers: for example, to direct a person to undertake work in the community, attend a drug rehabilitation course or pay a fine. The longest prison sentence I have passed so far is 20 years.

'Being a judge is different from most other professions because it can only be a second career. A judge first qualifies as a solicitor or barrister. Then, if they are successful in their career as a lawyer, they can apply to become a judge. This is usually after about 20 years in practice.

'My first career was as a barrister. I entered this profession because I had watched so many films and TV programmes about the drama of courtrooms and famous trial advocates. I was spellbound by the romantic notion of a brilliant advocate securing the acquittal of an innocent person wrongly accused.

'I did a law degree at university. While there, I undertook work experience in a solicitors' office and in barristers' chambers. This

> work gave me invaluable experience and fortified my view that I was destined for the bar.
>
> 'After university, I undertook the bar vocational course, which is the barristers' professional course. After that, I did pupillage, which is practical training through shadowing an experienced barrister.
>
> 'After 15 years as a barrister, I decided to apply to become a part-time judge. I was successful, and for 12 years I practised as a barrister, with occasional part-time sittings as a judge.
>
> 'Becoming a judge is a highly competitive process. The part-time judicial sittings helped lift my profile and eventually, after a number of unsuccessful applications, I became a full-time judge. Success in the interview to become a circuit judge really came from being confident in my capabilities, which involved careful reflection on my successes in the courtroom as a barrister.
>
> 'Aspiring judges should work closely with a senior lawyer or another judge on their application form. They will need to use a lot of examples to demonstrate the appropriate skills, and it is useful to find someone more senior to help you identify your strongest examples.
>
> 'Throughout your career – from work experience at undergraduate level to work as a lawyer – you should note down each time you have successfully achieved something on the job, such as communicating effectively with someone from a disadvantaged background. By doing so, preparation for interviews will be much easier!'

Tribunals

A system of tribunals operates alongside the court system. Each type of tribunal specialises in a particular area of law. For example, Employment Tribunals handle workplace disputes between employers and employees, such as disputed deductions from wages, unfair dismissal, redundancy and discrimination. A tribunal is a more informal setting than a court; tribunals are chaired by a legally qualified tribunal judge, who will often sit with specialist non-legal members who have particular experience in the subject matter of the tribunal. There is no standard form of procedure. Nonetheless, they operate in a similar way to court proceedings, with witnesses usually giving evidence on oath.

Reform

The English legal system is constantly changing, so it is very important you keep up to date with current affairs in the legal field if you are thinking about a legal career. Essential preparation for a legal career includes reading a good quality newspaper such as *The Times*. You can also look at professional journals such as *The Law Society Gazette* and *The Lawyer*, which are both available online. Further details and website addresses are contained in Chapter 12.

The Scottish legal system

Scotland has its own legal system, with significant differences from those of the other constituent nations of the United Kingdom. The two fundamental differences are the role of the Scottish Parliament in formulating legislation, and the basis of Scottish jurisprudence in a mixed system of uncodified civil law and common law.

Since 1999, the Scottish Parliament has been responsible for legislating on a wide range of domestic matters relating to Scotland, but there are certain policy areas reserved for the UK Parliament at Westminster. Notably, these include constitutional matters, defence and national security policy, foreign policy, and fiscal and economic policy. Scotland's legal system and court structure is separate and autonomous from that of England and Wales and Northern Ireland. Historically, it has its basis in Roman law, with some English common law influence since the Act of Union of 1707. Recent developments in Scottish law have seen the strong influence of English (and other jurisdictions') common law, as well as the influence and incorporation of European Union law.

While some areas of law are similar to that of England, Scotland has its own system of criminal law and procedure, of civil procedure, and of certain areas of private law (such as land law). The court system reflects these differences, with its own system of separate criminal and civil courts. By way of illustration, the Court of Session is Scotland's supreme court for civil cases and the High Court of Justiciary is Scotland's supreme court for criminal cases. Decisions of the High Court of Justiciary are not generally subject to review by the UK Supreme Court, which reflects Scotland's distinctive tradition of criminal law and procedure. Most cases in Scotland are dealt with in either the Sheriff Court, which deals with the majority of civil cases and more serious criminal offences, or the Justice of the Peace Court, which deals with less serious criminal offences. Tribunals also sit in Scotland. The legal profession in Scotland is outlined in Chapter 3.

The UK Withdrawal from the European Union (Continuity) (Scotland) Act 2020 was passed by the Scottish Parliament in December 2020 and gave powers to the Scottish Government to allow devolved Scots law to be kept aligned with future EU law. It came into effect on 29 January 2021.

For more information see: www.scotcourts.gov.uk/about-the-scottish-court-service.

The Northern Irish legal system

Like Scotland, Northern Ireland (NI) has a legal system separate from that of England and Wales. Unlike Scotland, NI's legal system to a large extent mirrors that of England and Wales, with the following differences.

In terms of legislation, the Northern Ireland Assembly (which gained legislative powers in 1999 following the Good Friday Agreement) has the power to make laws for NI on all transferred matters, which are generally in the economic and social field. The Westminster Parliament retains responsibility for matters of national importance, such as the constitution, national security, defence and foreign policy. The Assembly operates under a unique power-sharing arrangement between the two main political communities in Northern Ireland.

NI has its own judicial system (the Northern Ireland Courts and Tribunals Service), which parallels that of England and Wales. It includes the Court of Appeal, the High Court of Justice in Northern Ireland, the crown court, magistrates' courts and county courts. The highest court of appeal for both criminal and civil matters, as in England and Wales, is the UK Supreme Court. Judicial law in NI partially derives from English common law and is based on the doctrine of judicial precedent. It has developed along very similar lines to that of English common law. English precedent from the higher courts is not, however, binding, but is deemed to be persuasive. The higher Northern Irish courts also pay attention to important decisions made in the Republic of Ireland (ROI), the major Commonwealth nations and even the USA. The legal profession in Northern Ireland is outlined in Chapter 3.

The biggest legal challenge for Northern Ireland in the Brexit process has been the contentious topic of free trade with Europe and the legality of a hard border. The Northern Ireland Protocol was established to protect many legal challenges from the Withdrawal Act, especially those threatening the Good Friday Agreement.

On 27 February 2023, the UK and EU established the Windsor Framework, which introduced significant changes in three main areas: enhancing trade flow within the UK internal market by eliminating barriers that affected east–west trade, ensuring Northern Ireland's position within the Union, and tackling the underlying democratic shortfall present in the original Northern Ireland Protocol. These modifications were officially endorsed during the Withdrawal Agreement Joint Committee meeting on 24 March 2023.

Through this fresh agreement, the UK government reaffirms its enduring commitment to guarantee unimpeded and unrestricted access for Northern Ireland's businesses to their primary market in Great Britain while upholding their privileged access to the entire EU market. The Windsor Framework outlines a novel approach that restores equilibrium, which is essential for honoring the Belfast (Good Friday) Agreement across its various aspects. It implements a new legal and constitutional framework by amending the treaty text and eliminating several EU regulations.

For more information please see www.niassembly.gov.uk, www.gov.uk/guidance/devolution-settlement-northern-ireland and www.nidirect.gov.uk/information-and-services/crime-justice-and-law.

> 'Lawyers occasionally stumble over the truth, but most of them pick themselves up and hurry off as if nothing happened.'
> Winston Churchill

3 | A law unto themselves: What do lawyers do?

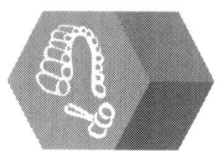

The legal profession in England and Wales is divided into two main branches: solicitors and barristers. This chapter will run through the working practices of each of the branches of the profession in more detail, as well as providing an overview of the legal profession in Scotland and Northern Ireland.

Solicitors

Solicitors' work is as diverse as life itself – they will be behind the scenes offering legal advice to their clients on everything from corporate takeovers to individual personal injury claims. The day-to-day tasks of a solicitor vary enormously depending on where they work. About 65% of all practising solicitors work in private practice for law firms: the rest work in-house either for companies or for government agencies. Even for those working in law firms, the work will be completely different depending on the type of firm. For example, in a large firm it is not unusual to be working as part of a team of lawyers on one large case for several months, whereas in a small firm you may have 20 or more cases on the go at one time and be solely responsible for dealing with these.

This section offers a brief overview of the different types of law firms and the sort of work that the solicitors who work in them undertake.

Large corporate firms

The largest law firms by turnover tend to be the big corporate law firms specialising in corporate and finance law, which usually have their headquarters in the City of London. Most of them also have large international operations. Data on these firms is collected and published regularly by the legal press and shows information such as turnover, number of lawyers employed and profits per partner.

There are broad categories into which these law firms are placed. There is a certain amount of debate about which firms should be in which category, and the precise picture changes annually, as some firms will grow faster than others, and the profitability of each firm will clearly vary year on year. There are also fairly frequent mergers between law firms. Therefore, all the categories in this chapter are broadbrush generalisations, and the lists of law firms within them should be viewed as illustrative examples only.

The Lawyer newspaper, which is available online, publishes a report in October every year on the top 200 law firms. The Legal 500 also publishes a directory of law firm profiles and this is also available online (www.legal500.com/law-firm-profiles). The general picture at the time of writing is as follows:

Magic Circle

There is a 'Magic Circle' of the most prestigious large international corporate firms which are based in London. The generally accepted view at the moment is that the Magic Circle firms are:

- Allen & Overy (2,800 lawyers) (merging with Shearman & Sterling in May 2024 to form A&O Shearman)
- Clifford Chance (3,300 lawyers)
- Freshfields Bruckhaus Deringer (2,800 lawyers)
- Linklaters (3,060 UK lawyers)
- Slaughter and May (560 UK lawyers).

The figures in brackets are the number of UK fee earners in each firm (comprising partners, assistants, trainees and legal executives) and are taken from The Lawyer Portal (free-to-source article resource) at the date of writing where available, or confirmed directly by the company.

These firms can offer great rewards, with high salaries and high profits per partner. However, the work often involves working long hours in a high-pressure environment. The first four firms have an extensive network of international offices, whereas Slaughter and May instead has strong links with selected overseas firms for international work. In general, many major London law firms have expanded considerably internationally.

Silver Circle

The term 'Silver Circle' was coined by *The Lawyer* in 2005, and refers to a group of elite law firms that are ranked just below the Magic Circle in terms of turnover, but still have considerably higher profits per partner and revenue per lawyer than other firms, together with a premium client base. These firms are also based in London, but most also have an international network of overseas offices.

The Silver Circle is a less settled group than the Magic Circle, but, at the time of writing, the firms within it are generally considered to be:

- Macfarlanes (527 lawyers)
- Travers Smith (220 UK lawyers).

In previous years, the firms Ashurst, Berwin Leighton Paisner and Herbert Smith Freehills were members of the Silver Circle, but have since followed international expansion strategies that prevented them from maintaining membership. Slaughter and May, Mischon de Reya and CMS have also been considered members of the Silver Circle in the past.

Although each of these firms falls within the top 50 for total revenue, they are quite spread out in terms of total revenue and are not simply the next biggest firms after the Magic Circle. The size and the number of international offices for each firm also differ. Macfarlanes and Travers Smith each have two offices abroad, while Mishcon de Reya has just one. It is important to consider that a global workforce will allow for trainees to experience potential overseas work.

Each of the firms within the Silver Circle has its own set of specialisms, but individual practices still span a wide range of jurisdictions.

American firms

The trend for large leading US law firms to open branches in London has continued apace and the largest US firms are now firmly entrenched in the UK legal market.

The US law firms with significant London branches include:

- Baker & McKenzie (530 UK lawyers)
- Kirkland & Ellis (340 UK lawyers)
- Latham & Watkins (480 UK lawyers)
- Reed Smith (321 UK lawyers)
- Shearman & Sterling (122 UK lawyers) (merging with Allen & Overy in May 2024 to form A&O Shearman)
- Skadden, Arps, Slate, Meagher & Flom (115 UK lawyers)
- Squire Patton Boggs (416 UK lawyers)
- Weil, Gotshal & Manges (169 UK lawyers)
- White & Case (316 UK lawyers).

Other major City firms

In addition to the Magic Circle and Silver Circle, some other large, well-respected City firms are:

- Ashurst (272 UK lawyers)
- Clyde & Co. (1,546 UK lawyers)
- CMS (1,072 UK lawyers)
- Dentons (602 UK lawyers)
- Herbert Smith Freehills (783 UK lawyers)
- Hogan Lovells (462 UK lawyers)
- Norton Rose Fulbright (816 UK lawyers).

3 What do lawyers do?

Major national and regional firms

If London is not for you, then there are some very large national and regional law firms with a major presence in large cities outside London. They offer the chance to do top-quality work with high-profile clients outside of London. Some of these firms have branches all over the country and many also have offices abroad, or associate offices abroad. These major national and regional law firms include:

- DAC Beachcroft (1,100 UK lawyers)
- DLA Piper (1,200 UK lawyers)
- Eversheds Sutherland (1,500 UK lawyers)
- Irwin Mitchell (1,105 UK lawyers)
- Pinsent Masons (1,000 UK lawyers).

What is the work like?

Large law firms tend to offer a comprehensive service to corporate clients, covering areas such as:

- company law
- mergers and acquisitions
- banking/finance law
- capital markets
- commercial litigation
- commercial property law
- competition law
- employment and pensions law
- financial regulatory law
- intellectual property law (i.e. copyright, trademarks and patents).

Work is often undertaken by teams, and the most junior members of the team may have little or no direct contact with the client. A typical area of work for a trainee involves conducting practical legal research or undertaking document checking work known as 'due diligence'.

Large corporate law firms tend to demand extremely high standards from their lawyers, who are well known for working long hours. In exchange, however, these firms offer excellent training and high salaries. They also usually offer good benefits, such as gym memberships, and also in-house catering services, possibly to avoid you ever having to leave your desk!

Most of the larger law firms will sponsor students that they have given training contracts to by paying their course fees for the Legal Practice Course (LPC) and Graduate Diploma in Law (GDL) (the postgraduate qualifications necessary to become a solicitor – see Chapter 4 for more details). In most cases, they also offer a maintenance grant to help with living costs. The grants vary considerably depending on firm and geographic location, and can fall between £6,000 and £12,000, though on average they tend to be around £7,000. For more information on the sponsorship and maintenance grants offered by solicitors' firms, visit https://targetjobs.co.uk/career-sectors/law-solicitors.

Starting salaries for trainees in City firms tend to be high, with typical training contract salaries for major law firms in London between £35,000 and £60,000 per annum, with the average salary being £44,858 per year. Many firms are now offering between £50,000 and £133,000 on qualification; however, for smaller firms outside of London the figures are not as high.

Usually, the larger law firms recruit two to three years ahead of when they expect the trainee to start work, and most will have a vacation placement scheme which typically takes place twice yearly, during the Easter and summer periods. As you can imagine, the large law firms tend to be massively over-subscribed. It is not unusual for a lawyer to leave a large law firm once qualified and move to a smaller firm for what is regarded as a better quality of life, due to shorter working hours.

Case study

When faced with the decision of choosing a course to study at university, Alex was still undecided as to what he wanted as a future career. It wasn't until after he graduated that he considered venturing into the field of law.

'When it came to choosing my university course, I decided to explore the academic realm that intrigued me the most – history. With an open mind, I pursued a degree in history, unsure about my future career path. After successfully graduating, I found myself at a crossroads, contemplating various career options. It was during this post-graduation period that law began to emerge as a compelling choice. To save up for postgraduate studies and reflect on my career aspirations, I secured a part-time administrative role at a small law firm.

'Working in this close-knit legal environment allowed me to gain a deep insight into the daily tasks and meticulous nature of legal work. The intellectual rigour and academic challenges that came with the role piqued my interest. After a year of immersion in this environment and valuable conversations with senior partners, I decided to pursue a Graduate Diploma in Law while continuing to work full-time.

'The journey into the world of law didn't come without its challenges. I soon realised that securing a training contract was highly competitive, and my limited prior experience in the field posed a hurdle. Nonetheless, my determination to succeed in law remained unwavering. Previous employers welcomed me back, granting me an opportunity to work as a paralegal, significantly boosting my exposure to legal practice.

'Regrettably, the small law firm where I previously worked couldn't offer me a training contract. However, after a year of dedication as a paralegal and volunteer work, I was fortunate to secure a training contract with another smaller firm. This choice aligned with my preference for a more focused training environment with a supportive network and a broader range of cases to tackle.

'Though still in the early stages of my legal career, I've already experienced working directly with clients. I find great satisfaction in the intellectual challenges of my work, appreciating how each client's needs demand a unique approach. Conversations with clients and broader legal discussions are particularly enjoyable for me.

'While my journey into law may not have been typical, it demonstrates that with hard work and determination, achieving your desired career is possible. To aspiring lawyers, my advice is to seek out valuable experiences early on and target firms that align with your interests. The unconventional route to success can be just as rewarding as the traditional one.'

Case study

Edward always knew that he wanted to pursue a career in the field of law, and had his sights set on being a solicitor. As he knew what he was working towards, he took meticulous steps to ensure that he could stay on track.

'I studied Politics, Economics, History and Law at A level. I had read that A level Law may be frowned upon by universities when applying to study it at degree level, but as I was already taking three other A levels, I felt it would be worth it in order to have a grounding in what I would be studying for three years afterwards. However, it didn't present any problems with my university application, and it actually led me to wider reading that I might not have undertaken otherwise. While my other A levels were not directly linked to law, I was always keen to try and identify where there was an overlap. By the time I came to apply for university, I felt I could discuss law in a number of different contexts by staying up to date with what was going on in the legal world. I hadn't been able to get any work experience before applying, but reading and visiting law courts certainly helped to fill in gaps. If you find yourself in a similar position, I would encourage you to access whatever you can online about the world of law and to speak to people working in the profession where possible.

'I ultimately chose to study LLB Law at the University of Sheffield. In the first year, we covered a broad range of content, including private, public, property, contract, tort and criminal law, as well as learning in depth about the English legal system and developing practical skills. In the following two years, there were core training and modules that were taken alongside a smaller number of optional modules. I chose to specialise in contract law, as it was an area that I felt drawn to and could see myself working in. The degree involved a great deal of independent reading. Some people can find this extremely tedious, but it can be fascinating. I also participated in law society activities that involved debates and mock trials. They can be daunting and uncomfortable at first, especially if you're naturally more introverted, but that makes it all the more important. Getting used to putting yourself out there can be invaluable later in your career.

'I was very fortunate to be in a position after graduating from my undergraduate degree with a 2.i to self-fund the LPC. I knew that I wanted to work for a big firm, and I didn't feel that my CV was strong enough at that point to apply for training contracts. I still applied that year in order to get experience of the application process, but opted to stick with my original plan of completing the LPC. I knew that the LPC was intense, so I wanted to make sure I could focus my efforts on that. At the same time, I also used that period to apply for a number of placements and schemes that could help me to develop my exposure, skills and experience. I was able to do a lot of wider reading about the world where law operates. I was able to fully immerse myself in the study of law, and while I knew having completed the LPC wouldn't necessarily put me in a stronger position for applying for training contracts, I felt more confident and worldly.

'After many applications, I was able to secure a training contract with a relatively large firm in Birmingham. The application process was tough and it can be really difficult to take the rejections at times. I also found it very frustrating when I didn't get feedback after a rejection, but I appreciate now that there would have been vast numbers of candidates to sift through. My advice is that if you get rejected at this stage, don't be disheartened – keep going! The interview process was extremely thorough and I think having the extra time to study and read and keep up to date with legal events put me in a much stronger position, even though my hands-on experience was probably limited compared to other applicants.

> 'Throughout my training period, I gained exposure to a number of different areas of law, including government, employment, contract, commercial and corporate. All of these areas had their advantages (and disadvantages), but there was something that drew me towards commercial law. I really enjoyed the ability to link my knowledge of law to the workings of a business, especially as the latter changes so often. It was an area that I found intellectually challenging, interesting and exciting, and I also enjoyed the prospect of a relatively stable career. On a day-to-day basis, I work with numerous clients with differing demands, and sometimes it can be just that – demanding – but I always find that the job satisfaction outweighs the complexities and long working hours. Being part of a big firm means that, with each year, I am becoming more specialised in what I offer.'

Smaller law firms

These make up the largest number of law firms, and range in size from one solicitor (sole practitioner) to firms with over 50 lawyers. They tend to specialise in areas more relevant to individuals than companies, or have smaller company clients. For example, on most high streets or in smaller town centres you will find at least one small firm dealing with:

- civil litigation (disputes between individuals)
- conveyancing (sale and purchase of property)
- wills, probate and trusts
- employment law
- family law
- criminal law.

Due to the location of their offices, these firms tend to be categorised as high-street firms – but remember that small firms can still offer high-quality corporate work if they have the clients, and every high street is surrounded by small businesses! Do not forget that most large cities will have many small commercial firms dealing with good commercial work, as well as true high-street firms which concentrate more on individuals. Larger firms may take half a dozen trainees a year, whereas the smallest firms may recruit trainees only occasionally as the need arises.

Typically a trainee solicitor in a small firm will have much more client contact from an early stage. You may still be working as part of a team, but normally you will work closely with the supervisor and, upon qualification, you will work autonomously. It is not unusual to have a high degree of responsibility, and even partnership, cast upon you early on.

The financial rewards might not be as high as those in the larger law firms, but smaller law firms tend to offer a different quality of life (such as shorter working hours) and work that is more related to everyday life.

The SRA's minimum required salary for trainees was scrapped in 2014 although employers must pay at least the national minimum wage. Typical trainee starting salaries outside of London are between £23,703 and £42,000, depending on location.

Usually small firms do not offer any support with course fees or maintenance, though there are an increasing number of exceptions. Most people who secure a training contract at a smaller firm will rely on scholarships and bursaries (such as hardship funds and the Law Society Diversity Access Scheme for those who qualify), loans (such as career and professional development loans), part-time work and family support to finance their studies. The support offered varies significantly between firms. It is also worth considering that at some institutions, the LPC and the GDL can be studied part-time over a two-year course, allowing more scope for part-time work and, ultimately, funding

Case study

When faced with the decision of choosing a course to study at university, Sam decided to pursue the academic area that he found the most interesting – politics – as he was unsure about what he wanted to do as a career. It wasn't until after he graduated that he considered venturing into the field of law.

'My interest in politics had led me to consider a number of career paths, including law, though it wasn't until I had graduated that I really gave it any serious consideration. Having obtained a first class degree in Politics from the University of Warwick, I undertook a part-time administrative role at a small law firm in order to save up some money for postgraduate study, and give myself some time to think about what I actually wanted to do.

'It was while working at the law firm that my interests started to drift towards working in law. Given the small nature of the firm, I was able to get a great insight into what it was that solicitors did on a daily basis, and the close attention to detail of the work and the academic rigour of the tasks really piqued my interest. After a year of working there and having had some incredibly helpful conversations with the partners, I opted to go ahead and complete a Graduate Diploma in Law at university while working full time. It was an intense year but I thoroughly enjoyed developing the foundation of knowledge required to practise.

'I had heard it was incredibly difficult to secure a training contract, but hadn't anticipated *quite* how competitive it would be. As I hadn't always been focused on this particular career path, I didn't have a great deal of experience, and this worked against me. However, I knew it was what I wanted to do and so I took it in my stride. My previous employers welcomed me back and allowed me to work as a paralegal which considerably enhanced my exposure to legal work.

'Unfortunately, the small firm that I worked for weren't in a position to offer me a training contract, but after a year of paralegal and voluntary work, I was really lucky to secure a training contract with another smaller firm. I opted for smaller firms because of the smaller trainee intake, allowing me to practise in a more focused setting with a greater deal of support, as well as the wider range of cases that I would be able to work on.

'Though I have only been working at the firm for a short period of time, I have already been able to work with clients directly and I don't think I would have had this experience at a larger firm. The work is tough and it is a steep learning curve, but I really enjoy the intellectual stimulation and how each client requires a different kind of support. I especially enjoy working with clients and discussing the legal components in a more broad manner. At the moment, I am just enjoying working through cases as they come, but I am hoping to become a partner of the firm in the future.

'Although my route into law wasn't typical, I was able to get where I wanted to be with a few years of hard work. My advice to aspiring lawyers who know what they want to do in advance would be to make sure that you get as much experience as you can, and target firms of particular interest to you early on in the process.'

Office-based or in the courtroom?

Traditionally, the work of a solicitor has been predominantly office-based, with some undertaking advocacy work in the lower courts, such as criminal work in the magistrates' court. This is still mainly the case as, in practice, solicitors can earn more money working in the office than they can waiting around at court for cases to be heard. In addition, the typical hourly charge-out rates for solicitors far exceed the average charge-out rates of barristers (for example, it is not uncommon for a junior barrister to earn as little as £90 for a solitary court appearance and £600 for a trial, whereas trainee solicitors, on average, may be charged out to clients at £200 per hour!) – so it is often more economical for the client if the soliitor instructs a barrister on their behalf to undertake court work.

Solicitors have been able to obtain the same right to be heard in the higher courts as barristers, known as the higher rights of audience. Once a solicitor has obtained experience of advocacy in the lower courts, they can undertake an additional training course and, upon successful completion of it, take up the higher rights of audience. A number of solicitors have taken this path and 7,157 practising solicitors are now able to represent their clients in court.

What makes a good solicitor?

Because solicitors deal directly with clients, perhaps the most important attribute required to make a good solicitor is excellent communication skills. Solicitors need to bridge the divide between the academic letter of the law and the practicalities of what the client is trying to achieve. The law needs to be explained to the client in terms they can appreciate and understand. Clearly, the demands placed on a solicitor in a large corporate City firm are very different from those placed on a solicitor in a high-street practice dealing with individuals, but all solicitors, wherever they work, will need:

- excellent communication skills
- the ability to cope with time pressure
- attention to detail
- good academic ability
- to be well organised
- the ability to work as a team.

Barristers

One of the complaints about the English legal system is that lawyers are like buses: as soon as one appears, another two or three turn up as well. This impression comes from the fact that solicitors can often instruct or retain barristers to give specialist advice or to represent the client in court – so, instead of hiring only one lawyer, the client now has at least two on their hands. This section will outline what barristers do and how their work differs from that of a solicitor.

What is the work like?

Barristers are specialist legal advisors and courtroom advocates: they are lawyers whom other lawyers consult on a specific issue, whether for advice or to make use of their advocacy skills. As suggested in Chapter 1, their work compares to that of consultants or surgeons in the medical profession, whereas the work of a solicitor compares more to that of a GP.

Just as the usual route to a consultant is through a referral from a GP, so the usual route to a barrister is through a solicitor (although there are a few exceptions to this): the Bar is a referral profession, so members of the public cannot generally directly engage a barrister. Solicitors will have good working relationships with barristers and are likely to know or be able to find out the most suitable barrister to deal with a particular case.

Barristers work as individual practitioners: most are self-employed and are responsible for their own caseload. They do, however, form groups, known as chambers, or sets, in which a number of barristers have their offices in the same building and share the administrative expenses of clerks and facilities – but these are not firms. Every chamber has an experienced barrister at its head; there will be a number of other members of varying seniority – permanent members of a set of chambers are known as tenants and temporary members are known as squatters.

Barristers are independent and objective, and will advise a client on the strengths and weaknesses of the case. Unlike solicitors, they automatically have rights of audience (the right to appear and present a case) in any court in the land. When a barrister qualifies, it is said that they have been 'called to the Bar', which refers to the bar or rail which used to divide the area of the courtroom used by the judge from the area used by the general public: only barristers were allowed to approach the bar to plead their clients' cases. The term 'barrister' is derived from this usage of bar. Barristers' seniority is measured in terms of their 'years of call', or how many years it has been since they were called to the Bar.

There are two types of barrister: senior counsel and junior counsel. Senior counsel are those senior barristers who have been made King's Counsel (KC) as a mark of outstanding ability. This is also known as 'taking silk', which refers to the silk gowns they traditionally wear – thus a senior barrister is often referred to as a silk. A KC is therefore a senior barrister who is normally instructed in serious or complex cases, and would usually appear only in the higher courts. Most senior judges once practised as KCs. Junior counsel is the term used to describe all other barristers who have not been made KCs.

Barristers tend to specialise in particular areas of law, for example civil law, family law, criminal law or immigration law. The work of a civil barrister may be divided into two types: contentious and non-contentious. Contentious work involves cases where litigation is contemplated or a real possibility. Non-contentious work involves advising on matters which have arisen not from a dispute between parties but often from a desire to avoid litigation in the future (for example the drafting of a will, the creation of a trust or advising on the terms of a contract).

Why engage a barrister?

A solicitor might want to engage a barrister for two main reasons. First, to gain an opinion on a matter of law from a person who is an expert or specialist in a particular field; second, to represent the client in court where the solicitor is not allowed to or would prefer a specialist advocate to take on the task. A well-argued case will impress a judge: good cross-examination will impress a jury. A barrister's specialist advocacy skills could make a difference to the outcome of a case.

When a solicitor asks for a barrister's view on a legal point it is known as seeking 'counsel's opinion'; where the barrister is asked to undertake litigation work (for example, disputes between individuals) in court it is known as 'instructing or briefing counsel', though the two expressions are often used loosely today. If an opinion is sought the barrister will be sent the relevant paperwork and will research the area of law and consider the issues before expressing a view as to the merits of the case or what steps to take next. In many cases, barristers are able to give advice on a case simply by looking at the papers. In more complex cases, and certainly cases which go to court, it will usually be necessary to have a conference or consultation with the barrister, typically at the barrister's chambers. If counsel is instructed to act, then the barrister will begin to prepare his or her arguments that will later be used in court. Thus most of a barrister's work will typically be centred on legal disputes. The barrister acts like the old medieval champion: stepping in to fight in the place of the client.

What makes a good barrister?

'You need to have utter confidence in what you are doing – or at least appear to,' says one young barrister. 'You are absolutely vulnerable to the whims of the solicitor. You need to be flexible and robust.' A key skill for a barrister is to persuade, so strong communication skills are high on the list. You also need to be interested in people and business, and to be commercially aware (you will, after all, effectively be running your own small business). Below is a list of skills and qualities you might need:

- strong written and verbal communication skills
- confidence
- energy and drive
- the ability to think on your feet
- flexibility and adaptability
- excellent academic ability
- independence
- interpersonal skills
- meticulousness and ability to master detail
- computer skills
- commercial awareness.

Indeed, the website of the Bar Standards Board (BSB) contains a health warning about the difficulties of getting into the barristers' profession (www.barstandardsboard.org.uk). This warning sets out the qualities that the BSB believes are required of a barrister, which are:

- have a high level of intellectual ability
- are highly articulate in written and spoken English
- can think and communicate under pressure
- have determination and stamina and are emotionally robust.

3   What do lawyers do?

Who works where?

There are over 13,500 barristers in self-employed independent practice in England and Wales. Although some do a wide variety of legal work, many focus on particular aspects of litigation and the law, specialising in areas such as construction, property, company law, crime, employment, personal injury, taxation, intellectual property and many other areas.

Barristers also work for the Crown Prosecution Service (CPS), the Government Legal Service and magistrates' courts. Some barristers may hardly ever appear in court but spend their time writing opinions and giving advice on complex and difficult areas of law. Most barristers practise from London but many are based in other cities and towns, including Birmingham, Bristol, Cardiff, Leeds, Manchester and Nottingham. All barristers who practise in England and Wales are members of one of the six legal circuits (geographical areas) into which the two countries are divided. The circuits are the areas around which the High Court judges travel to hear the most important cases.

Case study

Emily's journey unfolded from studying law at the University of Oxford to a rewarding and transformative career in a different field, all while being able to preserve the valuable skills that she cultivated during her academic pursuit. Emily's story showcases how her legal background now empowers her as a sustainability consultant, bridging law and environmental science.

'I began my academic journey at a reputable law school, filled with aspirations to make a meaningful impact in the legal world. I was initially drawn to law due to its captivating academic challenges. My dream was to become a barrister, fuelled by my deep passion for the subject. However, as I delved further into the world of law, I realised that it might not be my lifelong calling after all.

'In my final year of law school, I had a unique opportunity to participate in a legal clinic specialising in environmental law. Little did I know that experience would be the spark that set me on a completely different course. As much as I appreciated the significance of legal work, I found myself increasingly drawn to the broader context of environmental issues and the practical solutions that could address them.

'Upon graduation, I decided to embrace this newfound passion for environmental conservation and sustainability. I took a leap of faith and enrolled in a master's programme in Environmental Science and Policy. It was a significant departure from my legal background, but it was a decision driven by my heart's calling.

'I enthusiastically dived into research, fieldwork, and sustainability projects, becoming a keen advocate for environmental protection. My journey led me to internships with environmental organisations and government agencies, where I could make tangible contributions to sustainability efforts.

'Today, I work as a sustainability consultant for a global environmental firm. Having a Law degree served as a valuable platform for my career progression and contributed significantly to where I find myself today. My role allows me to combine the legal knowledge I acquired during my undergraduate studies with my new-found expertise in environmental science. I now advise businesses and government bodies on legal compliance, helping them adopt eco-friendly practices, reduce their carbon footprint, and implement sustainability strategies.'

Legal executives, paralegals and legal secretaries

Working alongside solicitors in firms are various other legal and support staff who are not fully qualified solicitors, but depending on the level of qualifications they hold may be able to carry out similar work to solicitors.

Legal executives will carry out many of the same tasks as solicitors, usually concentrating on one particular area of the law. They will therefore advise clients, carry out legal research and draft documents.

Paralegals (who may also be known as legal assistants) will work in law firms carrying out more routine legal tasks, including collating documents (for example putting together trial bundles), drafting more straightforward documents and carrying out legal research. Paralegals will often be law graduates who have not moved on to the vocational and professional stages of training. Working as a paralegal can often provide a route into becoming a qualified solicitor. The paralegal profession is currently not formally regulated, which means that it is not necessary to have any formal qualifications to become a paralegal. Nevertheless, paralegals working in law firms are employed by solicitors and therefore regulated by the SRA, although in practice, the SRA usually holds the solicitors responsible if any problems occur with paralegals, as they are meant to be supervised by solicitors at all times. However, owing to the hectic nature of a solicitor's job, increasingly intricate tasks are being delegated to paralegals who are seeing cases through from beginning to end at a much higher frequency. This is especially true of areas where the work involved is fairly repetitive and similar in all cases. The Institute of Paralegals, the leading representative body for paralegals in the UK, publishes a code of conduct, which is a code of best practice. It also administers qualifications for paralegals. For more information see www.theiop.org.

Legal secretaries are basically secretaries who work in law firms – they give administrative support to solicitors. This will include taking telephone calls from clients, typing up documents and letters to clients, invoicing clients, and preparing and filing legal documents. There are no formal qualifications required to become a legal secretary, but good typing, communication and IT skills are the qualities that any firm employing a legal secretary would look for. There are several bodies offering various training courses for legal secretaries, including the Institute of Legal Secretaries and PAs (www.institutelegalsecretaries.com).

> More paralegals are being recruited to do routine work. This is often seen as a way in for law students hoping to find training contracts.

Case study

After securing excellent A level grades in Law, Government and Politics and Business Studies, Ethan took up his place at Aston University to study Law, where he obtained a first-class honours degree. Since graduating, Ethan has taken on a number of roles and is now working as a paralegal for a large multinational law firm.

'I always knew that I wanted to study and practise law, and my A level choices helped confirm this decision. I chose Aston because of the outstanding reputation of its business school and the quality of working links that were promised. I enjoyed studying all of the modules covered, but especially equity and trust law, commercial law and intellectual property law. While I was at university, I was able to put my newly acquired skills into practice when advising students in the engineering department of their intellectual property rights, and I became heavily involved in a number of law-related societies, as well as making the most of guest lectures and networking events.

'After graduating, I knew I wanted to work in the legal sector, but I knew I still had a lot to learn before I would be able to make a final decision about the specific career path I wanted to pursue. The first role I took on as a graduate was as a legal assistant for a commercial company, and this involved supporting departments with clerical work that involved legal terminology and fact checking. I was also able to get stuck into contractual work by redesigning some of the contracts with international partner businesses and

> supporting staff with contractual arrangements with new clients. With the new GDPR laws being set out in recent years, I was also given the opportunity to work in a new role alongside the data protection officer at the company to redact personal and business sensitive data, conduct research into data protection topics to support the legal team and proposing alterations to existing contracts with business partners.
>
> 'I then decided to take on the role of a paralegal for a large law firm with many offices in the UK and abroad. I decided to target the paralegal role to continue to expose myself to a wide range of legal work, and the firm was an added bonus as their work is wide ranging, both in terms of their international impact and the multijurisdictional nature of the projects. In the short time that I have been working at the firm, I have had the opportunity to work with clients directly under the close supervision of a solicitor to build, maintain and develop helplines and billing processes; conduct research and analysis to generate metric reports and present them to clients during monthly meetings; and work with advisory bodies globally to ensure that international clients were working maximally to minimise the risk of disputes.
>
> 'At this moment in time, I am still unsure where my career will take me, but I am constantly seeking opportunities to enhance my exposure and develop my knowledge and skills.
>
> 'With a legal career, it is important to remember that things won't always go to plan – and it doesn't matter if you don't really have a plan! It is more important to be open minded when it comes to new roles and learning new things, as you never know where they might take you.'

The legal profession in Scotland

The main difference in the composition of the legal profession in Scotland is that instead of there being the two separate professions of solicitors and barristers, in Scotland there are solicitors and advocates.

Solicitors

As in England and Wales, solicitors in Scotland give advice on a wide variety of areas of law, with individual solicitors specialising in particular areas. Solicitors in Scotland can represent clients in the Justice of the Peace and Sheriff courts.

Solicitors in Scotland are both represented and regulated by the Law Society of Scotland, which sets standards for the profession, including education and training requirements, and disciplines solicitors where necessary.

Solicitor advocates

Solicitor advocates are experienced solicitors who have extended rights of audience and can also appear in the High Court of Justiciary and the Court of Session. They are members of the Law Society of Scotland and are regulated by that body.

Advocates

Advocates (sometimes referred to as 'counsel') are lawyers that are specifically trained in advocacy, so can represent clients in any Scottish court. They are equivalent to barristers in England and Wales, and the relationship between solicitors and advocates works the same as that between solicitors and barristers in England and Wales, in that advocates are usually instructed through a solicitor instead of being instructed directly by individuals.

Advocates are members of the Scottish Bar, and are regulated and represented by the Faculty of Advocates, which carries out similar functions as the Law Society of Scotland does for Scottish solicitors.

Reform of the legal profession in Scotland

The Legal Services (Scotland) Act 2010 made various changes to the operation of the legal profession in Scotland. It aimed to reduce the restrictions on solicitors entering into business relationships with non-solicitors, as the Legal Service Act 2007 has allowed solicitors, barristers and non-lawyers to work together in England and Wales. However, the introduction of so-called alternative business structures in Scotland has been long delayed due to a failure to introduce an appropriate regulatory structure. At the time of writing, despite the authorisation for the Law Society of Scotland to act as an approved regulator, the launch of that is still awaited and has stalled, supposedly because the Scottish Government have introduced a Legal Services Regulation Reform Bill and the Law Society are waiting to see the impact it will have on them.

For more information on the legal profession in Scotland see www.lawscot.org.uk and www.advocates.org.uk/about-advocates.

> **Case study**
>
> Nina's career in law is extremely wide and varied, and highlights that after qualifying, you don't have to stay in one lane.
>
> 'I completed my undergraduate degree in law at the University of Edinburgh, and, at the time, I was determined to work as a barrister. As such, I doggedly pursued this path and jumped through the hoops and over the hurdles that the path presents. After being called to the Bar, I worked successfully as a barrister for five years. I enjoyed the work – it was rewarding, demanding and rigorous, kept me on my toes and allowed me to carve out a name for myself. I loved law, though, and something told me I was missing out on something by not exposing myself to the work of a solicitor, so I decided to undertake the Qualified Lawyer Transfer Test (QLTT) to qualify as a solicitor.
>
> 'My main justification for doing this was that I wanted to use my skillset more broadly. I went on to work in the legal departments of a number of businesses, providing legal counsel and also contributing to sales roles because of my work approach. By developing my legal and commercial awareness in these roles, I was able to provide legal counsel for a number of company acquisitions worth billions of dollars, which took my negotiations global. In these roles, I was responsible for resolving all legal issues that arose globally through the acquisitions.
>
> 'I have since held the titles Head of Legal and Chief Legal Officer, helping to establish new companies, broaden their international impact and developing legal, marketing and public affairs teams. As with any legal role, no day is the same and the work is tough, but it is enormously exciting.'

The legal profession in Northern Ireland

As in England and Wales, the legal profession in Northern Ireland is divided into the two distinct branches of solicitors and barristers, and these professions have the same roles as in England and Wales. Solicitors in Northern Ireland are represented and regulated by the Law Society of Northern Ireland, and barristers are regulated by the General Council of the Bar of Northern Ireland.

For more information please see: www.lawsoc-ni.org/about-us and www.barofni.com.

4 | Above board: How to qualify as a lawyer

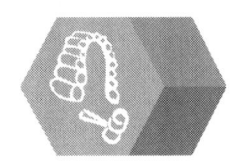

So now we come to the crucial matter: how do you start on the long road to becoming a lawyer? As there are two distinct branches of the legal profession, there are different training routes for each branch. This chapter will start by looking at how to qualify as a solicitor in England and Wales, followed by an overview of how to qualify as a solicitor in Scotland and Northern Ireland, and will then move on to qualifying as a barrister in each of the three jurisdictions.

Solicitors: England and Wales

There are a number of different routes to qualifying as a solicitor. Most of these are set out in the diagram on page 51 and then described in more detail in the text that follows.

Before university

A levels

A wide range of A levels provide an acceptable grounding for a law degree and there are no specific subject entry requirements to be able to study law at university. That said, there is clear benefit for (and an unwritten preference towards) those students who have demonstrated the necessary skillset through their subject choices. The traditional essay-based subjects such as History and English have an obvious appeal: they involve assimilating and analysing information, and a significant amount of writing, which will all be required on a law degree course. Languages may also prove to be very attractive to employers, particularly if you end up working for a firm with offices overseas, and sciences will develop logical thought and application, which are key skills for any lawyer. Many universities do not accept either General Studies or Critical Thinking A levels at all for any of their courses.

The website Informed Choices (www.informedchoices.ac.uk) outlines the subjects that might be required or be most useful for a chosen course, as well offering general guidance to those unsure about their future career paths. While it encourages students to choose subjects that they enjoy, the website suggests that 'essay-based subjects may be useful'. Aspiring lawyers should be aware that studying for a law degree involves a considerable amount of reading and research, requiring a high degree of literacy. Students who choose to study all maths and science A levels would not be penalised for their subject choices, but the volume and intensity of more essay-based subjects should not be underestimated; it may be advisable to practise these skills as much as possible in other areas, such as in the completion of the Extended Project Qualification (EPQ) or other extra-curricular activities.

The EPQ is an additional qualification, which requires you to undertake a self-directed period of research, which is then usually written up in a dissertation-style essay. This can be related either to one of your current A level subjects or to your future career, and could be a really useful way of demonstrating your passion for law.

Whether or not an aspiring lawyer should choose A level Law has, historically, caused some controversy – the key term here being 'historically'. The obvious advantage of taking law at A level is that it will provide you with an introduction to the subject and give you some idea of what studying law is like and whether or not it appeals to you before you have to commit to studying it at university. Previously, it was rumoured that studying A level Law could be held against undergraduate applicants, but this is not the case. Much of the discussion surrounding A level Law is based on its lack of rigour when compared to undergraduate study and, in this way, potentially being misleading. As with many A level subjects, the content covered within A level Law is brief and introductory, with students often finding the jump considerable. However, as long as you are prepared for the intellectual rigours of undergraduate study, choosing law as an A level subject should not be a hindrance. The bigger point here should be, if you already know that you wish to dedicate your life to this career, would you not rather find greater use in expanding your academic horizons, as opposed to becoming too focused on law so early on.

With all of your A level choices, it is important to choose subjects because you think you will enjoy them and they will play to your strengths. To be on the safe side, you should also take the following steps:

- if you already have a university in mind, check with the admissions section of its website to determine its specific entry requirements; and, if you wish to take law, whether or not it will be considered
- if you are already studying for your A levels but have not yet chosen which universities you would like to apply to, then do your research before applying so that you know which universities will accept your combination of A level subjects.

4 How to qualify as a lawyer

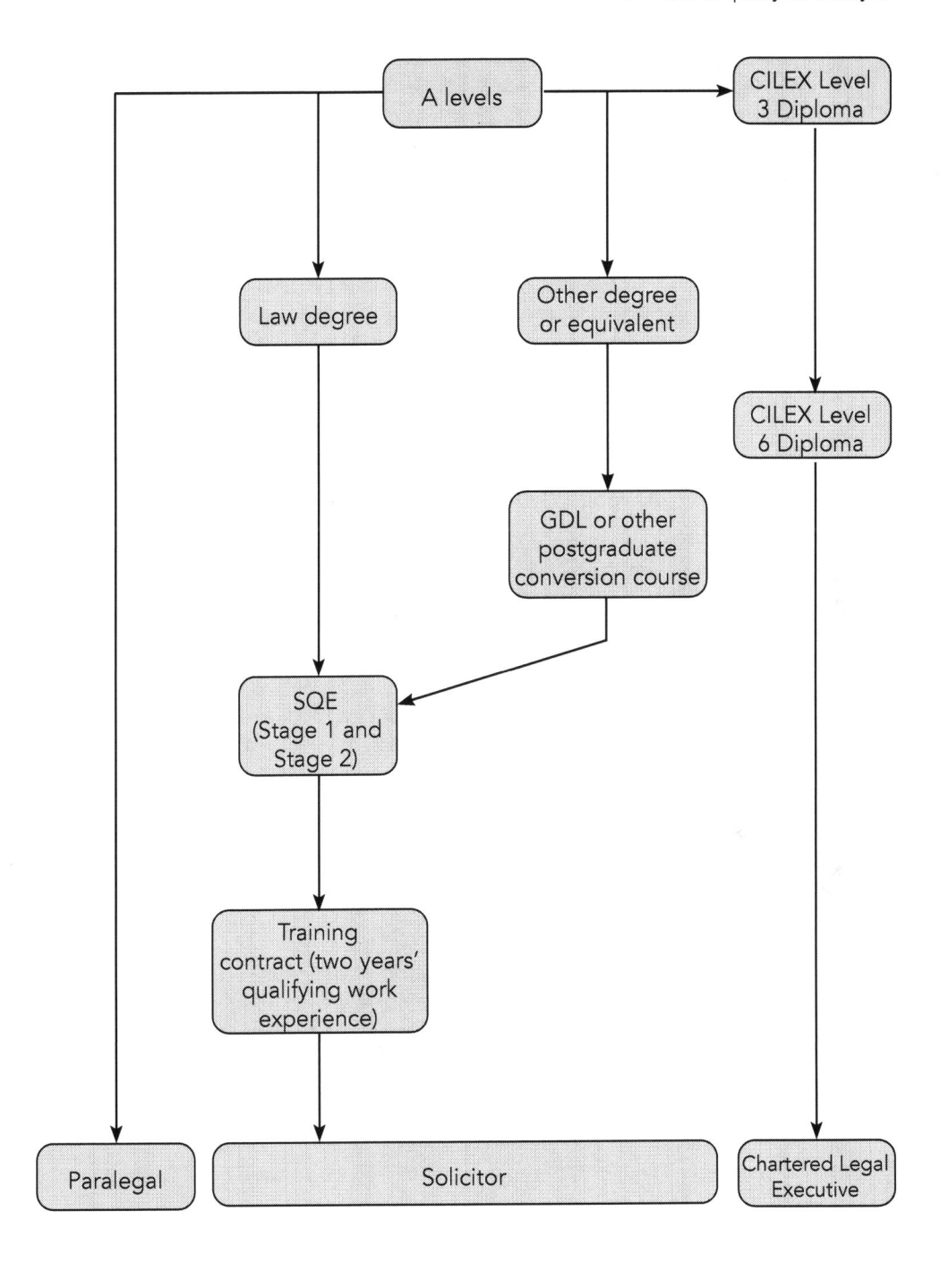

Figure 1: Qualification route for solicitors from 2021

UCAS advises that subjects such as physical education, dance, art and photography may not be considered as a suitable subject for one of the three A levels. At the time of writing, no UK universities stipulate specific A level requirements, but it is always worth checking before an application is submitted.

T levels

In September 2020, the government rolled out a new qualification in the form of T levels. A T level is a two-year course that follows GCSEs and is the equivalent of studying three A levels. The demands differ in that T levels combine classroom learning with a 315-hour industry placement in one of a number of subject areas, including legal. The closest option for students wishing to study law is Legal Services, which gives the core knowledge and skills to access a range of legal occupations. However, this is not a direct entry to university option.

Access to Higher Education courses

If you are a mature student who missed out on completing your secondary education, and cannot satisfy university entry requirements, Access to Higher Education (HE) courses are designed to help you move into higher education and on to degree-level studies. Most Access courses are delivered in further education colleges (although some are available at certain universities) and are available across England and Wales. The courses can be taken in a range of different subjects and lead to the Access to Higher Education Diploma, which is widely recognised by universities.

To find out more about Access to HE courses, visit the Access to Higher Education website (www.accesstohe.ac.uk), which contains further information on the Diploma and a link to a database of further education colleges offering Access courses.

Some employers will particularly welcome applicants who have had some 'life experience' in other fields before starting their legal career and the skills and qualities that more mature applicants offer can be much valued. This will be the case more for some employers than others (the civil service and teaching profession are good examples), although all employers must disregard age in their recruitment decisions to avoid breaking anti-age-discrimination laws. However, you should research the legal career you are interested in carefully before embarking on the expensive and time-consuming training to becoming a lawyer.

Degree-level study

Law degree

The most common route for qualifying as a solicitor is to pursue it as a graduate. Many people with an interest in law choose to study law at university, but this is not a requirement, and your first degree can be in any subject. Due to the recent changes in the pathway for qualifying as a solicitor, however, studying law at undergraduate level is a sensible option; the reality is, while the GDL tries to condense the knowledge into a year, there is little replacement for reading for the LLB over three years. The reason for this is that successful completion of the Solicitors Qualifying Exam (SQE) will require a good knowledge of law. It is also thought that many law degree providers will incorporate SQE preparation elements into their courses in the coming years.

Many universities offer law degrees, and these vary to some extent in style and content – for example:

- some are more traditional and 'academic' in approach
- some are slightly more vocational in outlook
- some enable you to obtain a joint degree (e.g. law and languages, law and politics, law and accountancy).

This variety gives you the opportunity to choose the degree that best suits your skills and interests. When identifying which universities to apply to, it is important to look at the specific modules and content that will be covered, as these can vary between providers, though there are some fundamental modules that tend to be covered by all. Further details regarding the types of law degree that are available are covered in Chapter 6.

Up until September 2021, there was an option to study a Qualifying Law Degree (QLD), as recognised by the Solicitors Regulation Authority (SRA). Having a QLD means that you have studied the subjects that the SRA considers to be the core foundation subjects for any lawyer. It is likely that many providers will still ensure that the core foundation subjects are covered within their law degrees, as these will help to prepare aspiring solicitors for the SQE, which is discussed in detail later in this chapter.

The core foundation subjects are:

- criminal law
- equity and the law of trusts
- law of the European Union
- obligations (including contract, restitution and tort law)
- property law
- public law (including constitutional law, administrative law and human rights law).

The SRA maintains a list of institutions and the degrees they offer that are recognised as QLDs, so if you want to pursue a degree historically considered as a QLD, you can check the list by visiting the SRA website (www.sra.org.uk/become-solicitor/courses/qualifying-law-degree-providers).

Once you complete your degree and enter the world of work, you will discover that many firms will expect you to have either a First or Upper Second class degree. You will need to work hard right from the outset of your degree to maximise your chances of getting a role with the firm of your choice.

Non-law degree

As previously mentioned, there is no requirement for your undergraduate degree to be in law, and you can pursue a career in law from a variety of backgrounds. Given that the SQE requires a thorough understanding of law, you may choose to undertake a postgraduate qualification in law, although this is not a requirement.

Historically, non-law graduates qualified as lawyers by completing the Graduate Diploma in Law (GDL) – although some universities and colleges (and indeed the SRA) still refer to it by its former name: the Common Professional Examination (CPE). This qualification is accepted by both the Bar Council and the SRA, so you could start the GDL without having decided whether you eventually intend to qualify as a solicitor or as a barrister, and then make your decision during the course of your studies.

The GDL is a condensed programme of study, usually comprising a one-year full-time course offered at around 50 universities and law schools across England and Wales. Many of the same institutions offer the GDL on a part-time basis over two years for added flexibility. Part-time online distance learning programmes are also available through some institutions, allowing students to work while studying. The SRA maintains a list of all institutions that offer the GDL (available at www.sra.org.uk/become-solicitor/legal-practice-course-route/qualifying-law-degree-common-professional-examination/cpe-gdl-course-providers).

Application for a full-time GDL course is made via the Central Applications Board (the CAB), which runs an online system similar to UCAS, acting as a hub for all full-time applications for the GDL and LPC. Up to three different institutions can be applied to at once. There are no application deadlines for the CAB, which simply recommends that candidates should apply at their 'earliest convenience', but it does advise you to check on the individual course providers' websites for application closing dates as they may not accept late applications. Applications for part-time or distance learning GDL courses are made direct to the institution(s) of your choice. Applicants must register on the website (www.lawcabs.ac.uk) and there is a £30 registration fee.

The current cost of a full-time GDL ranges from around £7,000 to around £14,000 (international students may have to pay higher fees). You should check what the course fee includes – for example, some providers will include the cost of all books and materials within their fees, whereas others will expect you to pay for these direct. You should also investigate the amount of contact time offered by the different course providers. Remember that you often get what you pay for, so do not necessarily opt for the most inexpensive course. Try to talk to some students who are currently studying or have previously studied at the institution you are interested in to find out whether they were happy with the course. You should also consider where you would like to undertake your work experience for the vocational part of the training, or which law firms you would like to work at in the future, as certain law firms favour specific law schools. For more information on funding the GDL, please see page 160.

Given that the GDL is no longer a requirement, a number of other postgraduate qualifications and training courses are also available that might provide a suitable basis of education for SQE preparation. Conversion courses such as the GDL are especially useful as they allow individuals considering a career in law who are unsure about whether to qualify as a barrister or solicitor to learn the knowledge and skills required for both pathways. Alternative qualifications range from postgraduate diploma level (PgDL) courses to master's level (MA Law) courses, of which there are many variations. Some courses will also incorporate SQE preparation, so if this is an important factor in your decision you should check the course content carefully. Other significant factors that might influence your decision include location of the provider, course content, course duration, flexibility and delivery type (i.e. self-study options and options for part-time study).

Case study

Jess didn't know what she wanted to pursue as a career, so opted to pursue a non-law undergraduate degree before undertaking a conversion course. She now works as a solicitor in employment law for a large firm.

'At sixth form, the prospect of choosing a degree to determine my future career was terrifying. I was interested in law as a possible option, but as I hadn't had any exposure to it at that point in my life, I was unsure about committing to it. At A level I studied English Literature, English Language, Geography and German. I also undertook an EPQ in a law-related area, and independently researched whether capital punishment should be reintroduced in the UK. English Literature was my favourite subject by far, so I decided to study that at the University of Bristol. I knew it would develop my skills in reading, writing and critical analysis, which would help to prepare me for a potential career in law if I decided to pursue it.

'While I was at university, I tried to make the most of the options available to me – I joined societies and attended lectures and workshops on a wide range of career options, but I especially enjoyed the law-related ones. I joined the Law Society, which allowed me to gain an insight into the law course, participate in mock debates, attend talks from law firm representatives and develop an all-round better understanding of what a career in law would entail, as well as what I'd need to do to pursue one. I also attended workshops on commercial awareness, leadership, negotiation and public speaking. The people I met through these activities led to several work experience placements with both small and large law firms over the course of my undergraduate studies, and three vacation schemes between my second and third year.

'I enjoyed these experiences so much that I knew the GDL was my next logical step. I maintained my attendance at Law Society events and got involved with any competitions that were taking place. I also provided voluntary legal aid for an employment rights service, which was invaluable experience, and piqued my interest in employment law. My undergraduate and postgraduate studies were an intense period, but it was well worth it and I enjoyed every minute.

'I was fortunate enough to gain a training contract with a law firm who offered financial support for the next stage of my training, the LPC. I studied the LPC with the University of Law over the course of one year. Once my training contract began, I rotated through four seats with a private client and then in commercial litigation, employment law and public law. Upon qualifying, I pursued a role in employment law, which means that I help clients with all legal matters that relate to employees in the workplace, such as dispute resolutions, contracting and managing relations.

'On a day-to-day basis, what you do can vary dramatically. Recently I advised a client on discrimination allegations, policy reviews in light of Brexit and an employee dismissal on the same day. You have to work with the facts, which requires a lot of skill that comes from legal training but ultimately, it all boils down to being good with people and having a high degree of emotional intelligence. When you are working with people, the same facts and laws can lead to very different outcomes, just because of how different people react. The other thing that I really enjoy is that employment law is always changing, which means that you're always learning to stay on top of the developments.'

Alternative routes into law

Non-graduate route

If you do not possess a degree, there are still a number of options available to you. You may apply to the SRA for a certificate of academic standing which will allow you to apply for the GDL course. This is granted by the SRA if it is satisfied that you hold other academic or vocational qualifications that it considers to be equivalent to a degree. Briefly, the situations where this may be possible include the following.

- **Mature students** – if you have a considerable amount of experience (normally at least 10 years) or have shown exceptional ability in an academic, professional, business or administrative field and have been educated to at least A level standard, and have a good command of both spoken and written English, the SRA may issue a certificate to allow you to take up a place on the GDL course.
- **Assistant Justices' Clerks** – clerks who have gained a Diploma in Magisterial Law are usually eligible to take the GDL, and may even be granted exemptions from some of the papers.
- **Chartered legal executives** – those already working in the legal sector, for example as a paralegal, could take the Chartered Institute of Legal Executives examinations during a period of qualifying employment. These qualifications are recognised by the SRA as being equivalent to a law degree and therefore enable you to progress to the next stage of training, the LPC (see below) without obtaining a degree.
- **Degree-level qualifications** – these may include professional accountants' or surveyors' qualifications.

More information on the non-graduate route to qualification is contained in the Academic Stage Handbook, which is available on the SRA website. If in any doubt, you should contact the SRA, whose staff will be able to give you advice on your particular circumstances.

Law apprenticeships

Aligned with the government's flagship campaign to promote apprenticeships, legal apprenticeships have increased in recent years. These pathways allow those who do not necessarily want to study at university – preferring to get stuck into the working side of the field – to pursue a career in law. There are four levels of law apprenticeship – legal administration, paralegal, chartered legal executive or solicitor – which can be completed as standalone apprenticeships, or can be studied consecutively to allow progression. The legal apprenticeships currently available include:

- CILEX Level 2 Diploma for Legal Secretaries: An introductory apprenticeship to secretarial work in a legal setting, which can be followed by Level 3 Legal Administrator Apprenticeship studies.

These apprenticeships typically take around 18 months to complete. Generally, the study content will be determined by the firm offering the apprenticeship, but will include broad themes such as legal text processing, principles of criminal liability, conveyancing, family law, communication skills, proofreading, minute taking and providing reception services.

- Level 3 Paralegal Apprenticeship: A two-year introduction to the background required for studying law, how this knowledge can be used in practice, how to conduct legal research and how to work with clients. It provides a solid grounding to allow progression onto the Level 3 Diploma in Law and Practice, or the Level 6 Chartered Legal Executive Apprenticeship. Day-to-day tasks might include the management of data and client records, the production of legal documentation, recording client correspondence, conducting research into the legal field for specific cases and communicating directly with clients.
- Level 6 Chartered Legal Executive Apprenticeship: A five-year programme that covers all of the qualifications required to work as a chartered legal executive. This pathway is only available to those who have a background in the field, either through completion of the Level 3 Paralegal Apprenticeship or Level 3 CILEX qualifications.
- Level 7 Solicitor Apprenticeship: A six-year Degree Apprenticeship that allows apprentices to obtain an undergraduate law degree and master's degree (LLM) with City, University of London or Northumbria University, as well as covering the content of the Legal Practice Course (LPC). This particular route is aimed at those who have completed A level study (obtaining grades BBB or above), or are currently working as paralegals or chartered legal executives. The overall study time is reduced for those who have completed the Level 6 Chartered Legal Executive Apprenticeship. After completing the Level 7 Apprenticeship, apprentices will sit the Solicitors Regulation Authority's centralised assessment and, upon passing, will qualify as a solicitor. For solicitor apprentices, managing your own cases is not uncommon, and this will involve research, interviews, advising clients, developing working relationships, producing legal documents, advocacy and negotiation.

These apprenticeships offer an incredibly exciting opportunity for school leavers to qualify as lawyers without having to study at university full time. A wide range of UK law firms offer these apprenticeships, which allow people to carry out paid employment in a legal environment while studying to acquire professional qualifications. While all apprentices are guaranteed the national minimum wage, many firms will offer considerably better pay, but this varies from firm to firm.

As well as the routes listed above, a number of other legal-related apprenticeships are available, including for training in occupations such as actuarial technicians, conveyancing technicians, financial advisers, insurance professionals, internal audit practitioners, investment operations specialists, paraplanners, probate technicians and taxation technicians. Similarly, in addition to the option of undertaking a Degree Apprenticeship to become a solicitor, wider Degree Apprenticeships are available in areas such as accountancy and taxation, actuarial work, financial services, internal auditing, licensed conveyancing, economics, banking management, senior compliance and risk, senior insurance, senior investment and commercial banking. While these are not specifically legal apprenticeships, there are strong law elements to each of them that may be worth considering. The UCAS website is an excellent source of up-to-date subject-specific information on apprenticeships and Degree Apprenticeships related to law (www.ucas.com/explore/subjects/law).

There is fierce competition for a relatively small number of legal apprenticeships. There is no centralised route for applications; firms must be contacted and applied to on an individual basis. For students studying A levels and looking to apply for Level 7 Solicitor Apprenticeships, it would be a good idea to research the available options in the summer between years 12 and 13, before applying in year 13. There are no fixed deadlines with apprenticeship applications and application requirements will vary depending on the firms that are advertising them.

Degree Apprenticeships and UCAS 2024

With nearly 60% of prospective students now considering taking an apprenticeship versus an undergraduate degree, UCAS now lets you apply for them alongside your UCAS application. With 20% spent studying and 80% of your time working, there is little wonder as to why apprenticeships are so popular: money. Legal apprenticeships are particularly highly sought after. However, it is worthwhile noting in advance where this apprenticeship will take you, and it is not into front-line law. To become a solicitor, especially a city solicitor, there is no substitute for an undergraduate degree first.

Solicitors Qualifying Examination (SQE)

In 2021 the Solicitors Qualifying Examination (SQE) was rolled out and changed the way in which solicitors in England and Wales qualify.

The SQE is a series of examinations that provide a centralised assessment route and eradicate the variable and inconsistent pass rates of the LPC due to differences between providers. The SQE will now start to replace the LPC, but for those who have already commenced training to become a lawyer, a transition period is in place to give them the option to pursue the LPC route if they so desire. The SQE is considerably cheaper, with the exams totalling £3,980 (independent of any postgraduate or SQE courses).

> **Summary of the new qualification route**
> - Undertake first degree or equivalent qualification (such as a Degree Apprenticeship)
> - If required, take an SQE Stage 1 preparation course (i.e. for non-law graduates)
> - Complete Stage 1 of the SQE
> - Complete Stage 2 of the SQE
> - Undertake two years' worth of legal work experience
> - Meet the suitability and character requirements of the SRA
> - Qualify as a solicitor

In order to commence the SQE route, a first degree or an equivalent qualification (such as a Level 6 apprenticeship or a Level 6 CILEX qualification) must be held. This condition can also be met through equivalent experience as determined by the SRA, and might be suitable for those who have been working in the legal profession in an alternative role, such as a paralegal, for a considerable period of time. For non-law university graduates, undertaking a postgraduate law qualification is advised to ensure that they have the thorough theoretical legal grounding required for success in the exams.

It is thought that, as the SQE rolls out, both undergraduate and postgraduate providers of law courses will start to deliver SQE-specific training. Many providers of law courses have also started to offer courses specifically for SQE preparation. For example, the University of Law have adapted their LLM Legal Practice programme to cover both SQE stages (SQE1 and SQE2), while their PGDL and MA programmes have incorporated SQE1 preparation. They are also offering SQEspecific courses, including SQE Law Online Essentials and SQE1 Preparation Courses (see www.law.ac.uk/study/post graduate/sqe/courses). The SRA has also published a list of training providers (see www.lawsociety.org.uk/career-advice/becoming-a-solicitor/solicitors-qualifying-examination-sqe/preparatory-courses), although it is important to note that they are not accredited or regulated by the SRA in any way. While these courses are available, the SRA states that preparatory courses are not a requirement, and that a candidate's education and training should be sufficient to provide them with the skills and knowledge that they require to pass the formal assessments.

The SQE is divided into two main components: Stage 1 (SQE1) and Stage 2 (SQE2), which are summarised in Table 2 opposite. Stage 1 should be completed before undertaking work-based experience, with Stage 2 being completed following the conclusion of work-based experience, though this is flexible providing that SQE1 is passed in advance of SQE2. There are two sittings per calendar year for each assessment (in spring and autumn). Assessment specifications for both SQE1 and

SQE2, as well as sample questions, have been published on the SRA website (see https://sqe.sra.org.uk/exam-arrangements/assessment-information). Candidates have a six-year window to complete the assessments, with three resit attempts allowed within that period.

SQE1	SQE2
Two functioning legal knowledge (FKL) assessments comprising 180 multiple-choice questions, covering: • Business law and practice; dispute resolution; contract; tort; legal system of England and Wales; constitutional and administrative law and EU law • Property practice; wills and the administration of estates; solicitors' accounts; land law; trusts; criminal law and practice Principles of taxation will be examined only in the context of: • Business law and practice and Property law and practice • Wills and the administration of estates Ethics and professional conduct will also be assessed throughout the exams.	Divided into two parts, which are then combined to give one overall pass mark: • SQE2 Oral: interview and attendance note/legal analysis and advocacy; assessed in four oral assessments over two days • SQE2 Written: case and matter analysis, legal research, legal writing and legal drafting, assessed in 12 written assessments over three days.

Table 2: Solicitors Qualifying Examination (SQE) stages

As well as passing SQE stages 1 and 2, aspiring solicitors must also undertake two years of qualifying work experience. Appropriate work-based training could be obtained in a variety of ways, including formal training contracts, working in a law clinic, undertaking an apprenticeship, working as a paralegal, or through a placement as part of a sandwich degree. A maximum of four organisations can be used to obtain this experience. In each instance, a supervising solicitor would be required to sign a declaration that the student had the opportunity to develop the competencies in the Statement of Solicitor Competence. The work-based training component is designed to offer more flexibility for solicitors, which is an exciting step given the difficulty in obtaining formal training contracts, though some larger firms have indicated that they are likely to maintain the traditional training contract format. A detailed summary of what constitutes qualifying work experience and the competencies that should be developed can be found on the Law Society website (www.lawsociety.org.uk/career-advice/becoming-a-solicitor/solicitors-qualifying-examination-sqe/qualifying-work-experience-qwe).

The final SQE hurdle is satisfying the SRA's character and suitability requirements, which involves an assessment by the SRA to ensure that those wishing to work as solicitors can do so. The SRA will look at criminal records, any involvement with the police, any evidence of cheating in an educational context or significant financial difficulties. All applicants for the character and suitability assessment must undergo a screening process, which includes a background check conducted by the Disclosure and Barring Service (DBS), prior to submitting their application. This screening process incurs a fee of £34.

The LPC will no longer exist beyond the 2025/2026 academic year, leaving the SQE as the only qualification route.

The most up-to-date information regarding the SQE is available from the SRA website www.sra.org.uk/become-solicitor/sqe.

Transitional Arrangements

Following the introduction of the SQE route of qualification in September 2021, the SRA put in place transitional arrangements for candidates who have already commenced their qualification to become a solicitor beyond this date, including anyone enrolled on a QLD, GLD or LPC. For those qualifying for them, these arrangements are in place up until 2032.

For these candidates, rather than completing the SQE, they must first complete the academic stage of training through either a QLD, exempting law degree (ELD, see page 64) or GDL (if they have studied a non-law degree at undergraduate level) before completing the Legal Practice Course (LPC) and obtaining a training contract. Details of these stages are outlined below. Candidates benefiting from the transitional arrangements are eligible to transfer onto the new SQE route should they wish to.

Legal Practice Course (LPC)

Following completion of the academic stage of training, aspiring solicitors can choose, instead of the SQE, to complete an LPC at one of around 35 universities and law schools across England and Wales. The LPC can be completed over one year full-time or two years part-time (in a variety of formats including day, evening or weekend study patterns). The current cost ranges from around £7,850 to around £17,950 for the full-time course. The specific fee you'll pay depends on the course you select and the location of your chosen institution. The yearly fees are less for the part-time courses.

The LPC is made up of a combination of compulsory and elective modules. The compulsory modules cover the subjects and skills in the core practice areas, including business law and practice, property law and practice as well as litigation, and these must be covered irrespective of where the LPC is studied. You will also take three elective modules

4 How to qualify as a lawyer

```
┌─────────────────┐ ┌─────────────────┐ ┌─────────────────┐ ┌─────────────────┐
│ Non-law degree  │ │ Mature students │ │ Degree-equivalent│ │Assistant Justices'│
│(or any other    │ │ with sufficient │ │ qualifications  │ │ Clerks with a   │
│ degree that is  │ │ experience and  │ │                 │ │ Diploma in      │
│ not a QLD)      │ │ general education│ │                 │ │ Magisterial Law │
└────────┬────────┘ └────────┬────────┘ └────────┬────────┘ └────────┬────────┘
         │                   │                   │                   │
         └───────────────────┴─────────┬─────────┴───────────────────┘
                                       │
      ┌────────────────────────────────┼────────────────────────────────┐
      │                                │                                │
┌─────┴───────┐              ┌─────────┴─────────┐            ┌─────────┴─────────┐
│Qualifying law│             │ Graduate Diploma  │            │Chartered Institute│
│ degree (QLD)│              │ in Law (GDL) or   │            │of Legal Executives│
│             │              │       CPE         │            │qualifications with│
│             │              │                   │            │  legal experience │
└─────┬───────┘              └─────────┬─────────┘            └───────────────────┘
      │                                │
      └────────────────┬───────────────┘
                       │
              ┌────────┴────────┐
              │ Legal Practice  │
              │  Course (LPC)   │
              └────────┬────────┘
                       │
              ┌────────┴────────┐
              │Training contract│
              └────────┬────────┘
                       │
              ┌────────┴────────┐
              │    Solicitor    │
              └─────────────────┘
```

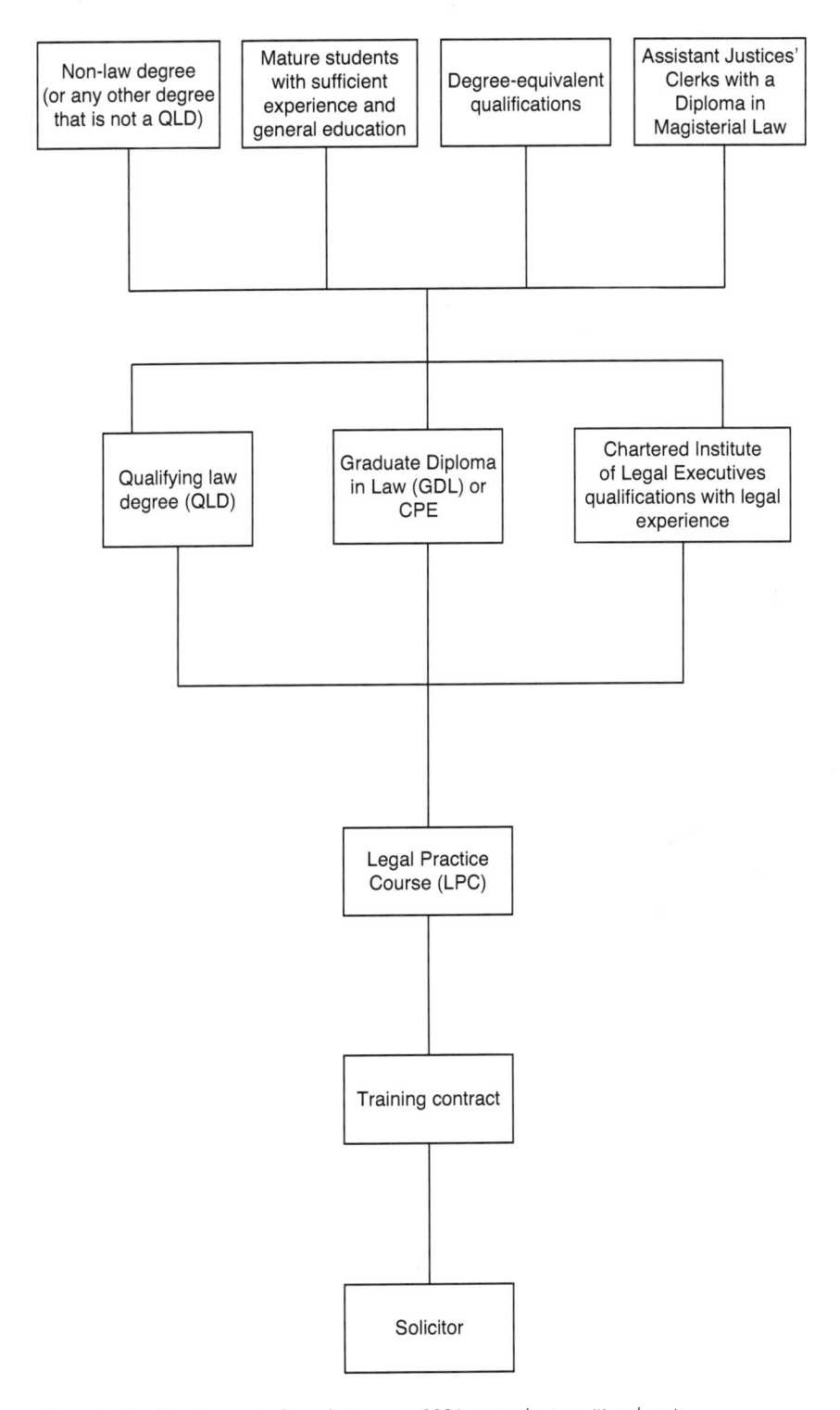

Figure 2: Qualification route for solicitors pre-2021 or via the transitional route

which you will be able to choose from the range offered by your chosen course provider. Different institutions offer different elective subjects, so when you apply for the LPC, you should make sure that you choose courses that offer the elective modules that you are interested in studying and pursuing as a career.

The larger solicitors' firms that offer help with fees for the LPC often only do so if you study for it at one of their preferred course providers and take the optional modules that are most relevant to their areas of practice. For example, if you intend to work in the City as a corporate lawyer, you will need to take commercial law options. BPP University has strong ties to the leading firms in the City and is the exclusive course provider for trainees from over 50 leading law firms. The University of Law is the preferred training provider for over 30 more law firms. You need to make sure that you take the LPC at the institution preferred by the law firm at which you would like to work.

The LPC is very different from the academic stage of training: it is based on legal practice rather than theory, and you will spend a lot more time in small groups with other students. The skills content of the course means you will experience much more 'learning by doing'.

As with the GDL, applications for a full-time LPC course must be made via the Central Applications Board (www.lawcabs.ac.uk). Again, the CAB does not have application deadlines for the LPC, but you should check with the institutions individually to see whether they have their own application deadlines. Applications for part-time courses are made direct to the institution(s) of your choice.

Exempting degree

The idea behind the exempting degree is to combine the academic and vocational stages of training. At the time of writing, only seven exempting law degrees are on offer. The universities that offer these are:

- Huddersfield University, Law (Exempting) Master of Law and Practice MLP
- Leeds Beckett University, MLaw: Law and Legal Practice
- Northumbria University, LLB Law Hons with Master's (Exempting)
- Pearson College London (validated by the University of Kent), M. Law Legal Professional Practice
- University of Central Lancashire, M. Law
- University of South Wales, M. Law, Legal Practice
- University of Westminster, Solicitors Exempting LLB Honours.

More information about exempting law degrees can be found on the SRA website (www.sra.org.uk/become-solicitor/legal-practice-course-route/qualifying-law-degree-common-professional-examination/exempting-law-degrees). The degrees are four years long and, on completion of your studies, you'll be deemed to have the equivalent of both a qualifying law degree and the LPC. The obvious attraction of the exempting degree can be the funding arrangements.

Training contract

The final stage of the traditional route to qualification as a solicitor is the training contract. This is (usually) two years of on-the-job training with a firm or other organisation which has been authorised by the SRA to take trainee solicitors. The purpose is to enable you to understand the practical implications of the law as well as developing your legal skills. The SRA requires you to gain experience in at least three distinct areas of law during your training contract and to further develop your legal skills while doing so. You should spend at least three months working in each of these areas. You will also have to complete the Professional Skills Course (PSC), which includes further training and some assessment in legal skills. Your firm or employer is expected to support you through this process and must pay your fees and reasonable travel expenses.

Depending on the sort of firm you want to go to for your training contract, you may need to apply up to three years in advance of your possible start date. This is certainly the case with the large City and national corporate and commercial firms, which will be recruiting as you are entering either the penultimate or the final year of your degree studies or starting your GDL. The application deadlines vary from firm to firm – some recruit earlier than others and some only have relatively short windows in which they will accept applications in any one year. Most recommend applying early. Other firms and organisations will recruit you as you are completing your LPC, with a view to an immediate start, so it is also common for students to start their LPC without knowing if they have a training contract to go to at the end of the course. There is a voluntary Code of Good Conduct for the recruitment of trainee solicitors, which represents good practice in legal recruitment. Law firms are not obliged to follow this Code, but most will in practice. The Code is available on the Law Society's website and specifies, among other things, that the opening date for training contract applications must not be earlier than the penultimate year of your undergraduate study. You cannot accept or decline any offers before 15 September in your final undergraduate year.

You can complete your training contract on a part-time basis and also combine your training contract with attendance on a part-time LPC. If you have considerable previous work experience in a legal environment, then you may be eligible for a reduction in the length of your training contract of up to six months, but this will depend on whether your employer supports your request. Any application has to be made to the SRA.

Competition for training contracts is fierce. Following the advice in this book should put you in the best possible position to obtain a training contract. You should also consider your A level choices carefully and obtain the best grades you can, as well as considering your choice of university carefully – there is some evidence that the top firms still look to what they perceive as the 'good' universities for their trainees. Finally, enrol on some vacation schemes and try hard to obtain some relevant work experience (see Chapter 5 for more details).

| Students enrolling on the LPC (2020/2021) | 7,338 |
| New training contracts started (2020/2021) | 5,495 |

Table 3: Competition for solicitors' training contracts (www.lawcabs.ac.uk and www.lawsociety.org.uk)

Funding your qualification

Qualifying as a solicitor can be an expensive business, and there is no funding available for preparation courses at the time of writing. The Law Society is currently lobbying for a source of funding for those in financial need.

For those undertaking postgraduate study or who are qualifying through the LPC route, some potential sources of funding are outlined below

Sponsorship

Most of the larger firms will sponsor you through the LPC, and possibly the GDL, if you have secured your training contract before commencing the course. The sponsorship will cover the cost of the GDL/LPC course fees and usually a contribution towards your living expenses as well. You'll need to check whether the firms that interest you would offer sponsorship of this kind. Firms providing sponsorship deals often do so on the proviso that you take your LPC at their preferred university or college. This is so that they can make sure that you study the subjects that they will need you to know about once you start working for them.

While there is now a postgraduate loan available of £12,167 (www.gov.uk/funding-for-postgraduate-study) to those who do not hold any postgraduate qualifications, these are typically not available for the GDL or LPC (the GDL is a diploma and the LPC is a certificate). However, some LPCs now include a master's qualification, which qualifies them for the loan.

There are some private student loan providers, such as Future Finance loans, and graduate bank loans that can also be explored.

Law Society Diversity Access Scheme

The Law Society has a Diversity Access Scheme (DAS), which is aimed at students from disadvantaged backgrounds or those who face exceptional obstacles to qualification. Applicants must meet several of the listed criteria, which include aspects such as:

4 How to qualify as a lawyer

- no access to familial loans or financial gifts
- no access to more than £5,000 in savings accounts, current accounts or ISAs
- attended a non-fee-paying school
- part of the first generation of the family to have attended higher education
- recipient of free school meals during compulsory-aged education
- exceptional circumstances relating to gender, ethnicity, sexual orientation, health, disability, educational or other personal obstacles.

Its purpose is to increase social diversity in the legal profession. The DAS offers payment of LPC course fees, plus the provision of work experience and a professional mentor.

The scheme is, however, extremely limited: in 2022, the Law Society received 216 applications, shortlisted 33 applications, and offered 15 DAS awards. The scheme also guarantees a training contract at a national law centre. Applications are typically accepted between February and April each year, and students are required to reflect on their financial situation, their desire to become a solicitor, the contributions they could make, current affairs and their work experience to date. Competition for awards is keen and applicants must have a confirmed place on the LPC.

More details are available on the Law Society's website (www.lawsociety.org.uk/campaigns/diversity-access-scheme).

Access funds and scholarships

These are available at some universities offering the LPC. Access funds may be available at publicly funded colleges and are discretionary awards aimed at assisting with your living costs if you are experiencing financial hardship. Scholarships may be awarded by any of the universities or colleges offering the LPC to students with particularly good academic backgrounds. Details are available direct from your institution of study.

Payment by instalments

Some institutions where you can take the LPC course offer the option to pay by instalments. You should check the institutions' individual websites for details.

Charities and grant-making trusts

Some grant-making trusts and charities may offer financial assistance to those seeking to qualify as a lawyer. You should search online to see whether you meet their criteria for an award, as these can be very specific.

Study part-time

More and more students are completing their professional training part-time, mostly due to the lack of financial support. This will enable you to work part-time to help support yourself. You should, however, make sure that you allow yourself enough time to study so that you pass the course.

Funding: conclusion

When you are looking for sources of funding, remember:

- do your research
- plan ahead
- read the criteria for any grant/award you are applying for very carefully and make sure you can demonstrate that you meet them
- don't be put off – you're hoping to train to be a solicitor so try to come up with a good case for yourself
- be realistic.

> **Case study**
>
> Sarah works as a self-employed barrister in Northern Ireland, and serves as a visiting lecturer at multiple esteemed universities.
>
> 'My journey into the legal field was quite the twist in my career path. When I was younger, I thought I wanted to work in accounting and finance, which led me to pursue an undergraduate degree in finance at Queen's University Belfast. On graduating, I landed a job at an accounting firm, where I found myself increasingly drawn to the legal proceedings taking place around me. It was through conversations with the firm's legal team and the chance to shadow their work that I made a pivotal decision.
>
> 'To transition into the world of law, I enrolled in a law conversion course at BPP Law School and followed that up with the Postgraduate Diploma in Professional Legal Studies (Bar). The academic training for law was incredibly rigorous, involving extensive readings and case studies. Admittedly, I encountered some rather dull aspects of the coursework, but here's a piece of advice: if you find some areas less engaging, don't be discouraged. You'll naturally discover your preferences and areas of interest. Personally, I found myself most captivated by constitutional and public law, two areas I've since specialised in, both in my legal practice and as a lecturer.
>
> 'After being called to the Bar, I embarked on a challenging 12-month pupillage. This experience was a steep learning curve, but it was also profoundly rewarding. It allowed me to put my knowledge into action and observe the legal system in full operation. Initially, taking on my own cases was a nerve-wracking experience, but I quickly learned that thorough preparation was the secret to overcoming those initial jitters and achieving success in my legal career.'

Solicitors: Scotland

The legal system in Scotland differs from that of England and Wales and Northern Ireland, and so does the qualification route. This section aims to summarise the process of qualifying as a solicitor in Scotland.

Briefly, the route to qualification involves studying for a four-year law degree in Scots Law at a Scottish university and then proceeding to the vocational training stage – the Diploma in Professional Legal Practice. There is no equivalent of the GDL in Scotland, so it is slightly more difficult to become a lawyer if your degree is in a subject other than law, as this necessitates taking a two-year accelerated law degree after your first degree. Further details on qualifying in Scotland are available on the Law Society of Scotland's website (www.lawscot.org.uk/members/business-support/recruitment-guidance/overview-of-the-route-to-qualification).

Academic stage

Law degree

It is possible to study a Bachelor of Law degree (LLB) at the following Scottish universities:

- University of Aberdeen
- University of Abertay
- University of Dundee
- University of Edinburgh
- Edinburgh Napier University
- Glasgow Caledonian University
- University of Glasgow
- Robert Gordon University
- University of Stirling
- University of Strathclyde.

More detailed information about the content of the courses can be obtained from the universities' websites.

A law degree from an English university will not be accepted as a QLD in Scotland, and vice versa. However, if you have qualified in England, Wales, Northern Ireland or the European Union, there are transfer tests available in order to requalify in Scotland.

In November 2019, the Law Society of Scotland introduced the Qualified Lawyers Assessment (QLA), which is a universal set of exams that allows solicitors who qualified outside of Scotland to work there. Depending on prior training, there may be some exemptions from the 11 subjects that must be assessed through the exams. Potential candidates must first apply for the QLA to determine whether they are eligible. Further information about the exams can be found on www.lawscot.org.uk.

The non-graduate route

Alternatively, there is a non-degree route where someone who has been working as a full-time pre-Diploma trainee with a qualified solicitor in Scotland for three years can take the Law Society of Scotland's examinations and then proceed to the vocational stage of training in the same way as a law graduate. This route is known as the Pre-PEAT Training Contract and LSS exams, and, according to the Law Society of Scotland, is followed by between 10 and 20 people each year. For more information please see www.lawscot.org.uk/members/business-support/recruitment-guidance/overview-of-the-route-to-qualification.

Vocational stage

Diploma

After completion of the LLB degree all aspiring Scottish solicitors are required to take the Diploma in Professional Legal Practice (DPLP) which is also known as the Professional Education and Training Stage 1 (PEAT 1). It is usually taught full-time over one academic year, though some two-year part-time courses are also available. These can be studied at:

- University of Aberdeen
- University of Dundee
- University of Edinburgh
- University of Glasgow
- Robert Gordon University
- University of Strathclyde (over two years part-time).

The DPLP is the equivalent of the LPC in England and Wales, in that the course has been designed to teach the practical knowledge and skills necessary for the working life of a solicitor. The focus is highly practical and skills-based. To obtain a place on the diploma course, applicants would need to have passed all of the Law Society of Scotland's 'professional subjects' in their LLB (or Law Society examinations). Applications are made through UCAS between February and April each year.

At each institution, the content will be similar but the compulsory and elective modules on offer may vary, so research ahead of the application is advised to ensure that the most appropriate courses are selected. The Law Society of Scotland runs a Virtual Diploma Fair each year in January or February to allow providers to be compared.

Training contract

After successful completion of the degree (or non-graduate route) and diploma, you need to serve a two-year post-diploma training contract (Professional Education and Training Stage 2, or PEAT 2) with a practising solicitor in Scotland. This can be served with solicitors in private practice, the Crown Office, or local authorities and certain public bodies. The training contract is very similar to that in England and Wales, giving trainees the chance to put into practice what they have learnt at university. At the end of the two years, if the training contract has been successful then the trainee is qualified and can apply for a full practising certificate. As in England and Wales, competition for training contracts is intense and there are now fewer trainee roles available for a similar number of students passing the DPLP. A good academic profile is therefore important and the benefits of having obtained some work experience, particularly in the legal sector, cannot be over-estimated.

Case study

Stewart works as a solicitor in Scotland at an accident and injury claims firm. His route into law was long-winded and undoubtedly tough, but his perseverance paid off!

'I grew up in quite a rough part of Edinburgh, the kind of area where aspirations are thin on the ground and very few prosper due to lack of hope, money and opportunity. In short, I left school with no qualifications. I was told by my teachers at a very early age that I would not amount to much in life and I believed them. I eventually left school with nothing to show for my time there and a paper round that yielded £7 per week. I later took up a part-time job in a local music store but despite my best efforts, no full-time roles became available for me. I had a friend who worked in a solicitors' firm as an Office Junior and one day, he mentioned that there was a position available. I applied but was once again met with rejection, until I eventually received my stroke of luck – the person who had taken the position initially left after just a few weeks, so the job was mine!

'The solicitors' firm was a small trade union firm where I worked as an Office Junior in the Filing Department. I loved it – one of the perks of working for a small firm is that it feels as though you are working with a big family! From filing I moved onto data processing, before eventually being promoted to the role of Executive in Information Technology, which was a position I maintained for a number of years. To earn some extra money, I took on a part-time job as a barman. It was while working in the bar after a day at the office that I had a bit of an epiphany – I was working with the next generation of lawyers who were not much smarter than me. I decided to go for broke and see whether I could qualify as a lawyer myself.

'I contacted the Law Society to find out what was required and it was contingent on a lot of things coming together: primarily, consent from my employers, attending night school to get higher

Getting into Law

> academic grades, then passing nine exams before applying to do the diploma. I then approached one of the partners to gauge his views and, like many other times in my life, he told me he didn't think I was up to it. I was deflated somewhat but not deterred, and instead approached the most senior partner in the firm. To my surprise, he completely supported my decision and told me to return after I'd completed my exams so that I could talk to the partners. He was true to his word, and the company then supported me through the Law Society exams while allowing me to work as a pre-diploma trainee.
>
> 'This was a tough undertaking and I had to give up a lot – football, seeing my friends and family – as it meant long working hours, seven days a week, for four years. I was handed a syllabus but, other than that, no direction at all – there were no lectures or tutors, just huge piles of books! One of the stipulations from the Law Society was that all exams had to be passed within four sittings. By the end of the fifth year of studying, I had passed every exam other than the nemesis of taxation, in which I was about to undertake my fourth attempt at the exam. Having done so, I received a call to say I had failed. I was heartbroken and the Law Society bluntly told me I was out of options. I contacted directly each of the universities offering the diploma, but despite my pleas, they all closed the door. A glimmer of hope came from Alan Barr at the University of Edinburgh, who suggested I sit the taxation exam at undergraduate level the following term and, if I passed, he would allow me to study the diploma. I took him up on his offer and really couldn't believe how easy the exam was – the lecturers were incredibly helpful and I passed the exam, allowing me to ultimately qualify as a solicitor.'

Solicitors: Northern Ireland

The system for qualifying as a solicitor in Northern Ireland is different again from those in England, Wales and Scotland. Below is a brief summary, but further details can be obtained from the Law Society of Northern Ireland's website (www.lawsoc-ni.org/becoming-a-solicitor).

Academic stage

The usual route to qualification as a solicitor in Northern Ireland begins with a law degree. This must be considered by the Law Society of Northern Ireland to be a 'recognised law degree', and must contain eight core subjects. These are:

4 How to qualify as a lawyer

- law of evidence
- land law
- European law
- equity
- constitutional law
- law of tort
- law of contract
- criminal law.

Further details of what constitutes a recognised law degree, and a list of recognised law degrees and the universities offering them, are available on the website of the Institute of Professional Legal Studies, part of Queen's University Belfast (the 'Institute'). This list of recognised law degrees contains many from English and Welsh universities, as well as some in the Republic of Ireland, so this part of the route to qualification does not have to be taken in Northern Ireland. Degrees in Scottish law are not, however, recognised.

Students with non-law degrees can also qualify as a solicitor by first taking the master's in Law at Queen's University Belfast. This is an accelerated, fast-track programme that lasts two years when studied full time.

There is also an alternative, non-degree route available. Typically, these individuals must have qualifications that render them suitable for consideration (i.e. the same as those required for a place at Queen's University Belfast), and would usually be over 30 years of age. Please visit the website of the Law Society of Northern Ireland (www.lawsoc-ni.org/becoming-a-solicitor) for further details.

Vocational stage and apprenticeship

The vocational training to become a solicitor in Northern Ireland (the Postgraduate Diploma in Legal Practice) is undertaken at the Institute. All applicants applying for the diploma must sit an entrance exam in the December before they wish to commence the course (known colloquially as the 'Institute exam'). Applications must be submitted to the Institute by 15 November in the relevant year. The main difference from the system in England and Wales is that applicants must have already found a master (a solicitor with whom the applicant proposes to serve his/her on-the-job training, known as the apprenticeship) by the time they apply for the vocational course. The vocational course is then combined with the apprenticeship. Finding a master can be a difficult and competitive process.

The apprenticeship is similar to a training contract in England and Wales, in that it will last for two years for trainees who completed the traditional qualification route. However, in order to combine it with the vocational training, each year is structured as follows.

- September to December: spent in-office.
- January to December: spent at the Institute of Professional Legal Studies (but returning to master's office during vacations).
- January to August: spent in-office.

Once a trainee has passed all the relevant examinations and completed their apprenticeship, they can apply to be enrolled as a solicitor of the Court of Judicature in Northern Ireland and apply for a Practising Certificate. A restricted practising certificate is issued for the first two or three years, meaning that newly qualified solicitors can only practise as employees within a firm of solicitors and cannot set up their own practice.

For more information on qualifying as a solicitor in Northern Ireland, please see www.lawsoc-ni.org/becoming-a-solicitor.

Case study

Andrew is a solicitor at the Law Society of Northern Ireland. He followed a relatively straightforward route into law and has amassed a range of experience in different areas of law.

'At the age of 17, I took on a month-long placement at my family's solicitors' firm in my home town of Coleraine. It was a typical small country practice with three solicitors dealing with all different types of work. I experienced a variety of cases including criminal, conveyancing, personal injury, Children Order, family and administration of estates. It also gave me the opportunity to sit in on police interviews, court hearings and meet the local judge in chambers. This was my first real introduction into the field of law.

'Shortly afterwards, I commenced my A level studies in economics, maths and politics, securing grades ABB. This was sufficient to get me into Queen's University Belfast, to study law. I decided upon a law degree because I thought it was a good general degree to have. I did not have any burning desire to do anything in particular so was essentially trying to cover my bases! I knew I would pick up a wealth of transferable skills that would be beneficial regardless of what I decided to do after graduating.

'The degree was very much the traditional three-year law degree that covered each of the core areas. While I was academically capable, I found the course quite dry and still hadn't really pinned down what I wanted to do with my life. At the end of my degree, I worked for a summer in an accountants' firm while also putting in my application to the Institute of Professional Legal Studies (IPLS) in Belfast. The IPLS works on the basis that you must obtain a master's degree, so I got a place in a solicitors' firm in Belfast. The term commenced with a full-time placement in the office followed by lessons at the IPLS. The course itself was a mixture of lectures and small group study sessions. It also incorporated practical exercises, such as mock bail applications and client interviews. This course offered a much more practical introduction to the day-to-day work of a solicitor than the undergraduate degree course.

'I worked in corporate and commercial law for nine months after qualifying. I did not particularly enjoy this type of work so I moved to another firm to do property and private client work. This work was much more to my liking and I stayed there for several years until I joined the Law Society. During my time at the property firm, I became a member of the Society of Trust and Estate Practitioners.

'My experience in private practice was challenging, particularly on the property side. With the property crash from July 2007, there were a number of rounds of redundancies which I thankfully managed to avoid, mostly due to being the only solicitor in the firm who did private client work. I acted for a large number of property developers, some of whom went bust during those years so there was very little work around. My private client work basically supported my property work during this time. The commercial realities of life in private practice were reinforced at this time. Billing, outstanding costs and cashflow became even more vital than previously.

'I moved to the Law Society to deal with all non-contentious work. I am secretary to the Conveyancing & Property Committee, Non-Contentious Business Committee and the Human Rights & Equality Committee, among other duties. The work is challenging but interesting. In particular, I am currently dealing with the review of the Home Charter Scheme (the Northern Irish equivalent of the QCS which has been in place since 1994); this means servicing four additional sub-committees and dealing with all the technical drafting that is produced. The most difficult but most interesting part of this is the review of the General Conditions of Sale (the NI standard property contract). I also give seminars to our members on a variety of subjects. I will have done 15 seminars this year around the province. The job is not like any other, but I find it interesting and it has certainly given me a much wider understanding of the issues facing the legal system in Northern Ireland, including regulatory issues and statutory issues.'

Barristers: England and Wales

Academic stage

The academic stage of training required to become a barrister is the same as that to become a solicitor. It is only once a student reaches the vocational stage of training that the qualification routes for solicitors and barristers diverge. A good academic background is even more important for aspiring barristers than it is for solicitors: it will be very difficult to obtain a pupillage unless you achieve at least an Upper Second class degree.

Vocational stage

New pathways to qualifying

To become a barrister entitled to practise, the Bar Council requires you to have completed a stage of academic training, followed by vocational training and then the completion of a pupillage. Historically, the vocational stage of training involved completing the Bar Professional Training Course (BPTC), which is still an option, but the Bar Standards Board have recently outlined alternative pathways to qualifying. These include:

- **Three-step pathway.** This involves an academic component, followed by a vocational component and, finally, a pupillage or work-based component.
- **Four-step pathway.** This involves an academic component, followed by a vocational component in two parts, and then a pupillage or work-based component.
- **Integrated academic and vocational pathway.** This combines academic and vocational components, which are then followed by a pupillage or work-based component.
- **Apprenticeship pathway.** This combines academic, vocational and pupillage components.

The BPTC option is the most long-standing and, therefore, well-established three-step pathway, which many aspiring barristers will continue to pursue. However, it is important to note that alternative options are becoming available and these are likely to become more widely accessible in the coming years.

The Authorised Education and Training Organisations (AETOs) and the Bar training that they have been authorised by the Bar Standards Board to deliver from September 2020 are summarised in the table below. At the time of writing, there are no established providers of the apprenticeship pathway, but AETOs have been invited to submit proposals. As such, apprenticeships for barristers may be an option in the coming years.

Bar training provider	Components delivered
BPP University	Vocational component of the three-step pathway Vocational component of the four-step pathway (delivered in two parts) Academic and vocational components of the integrated pathway
Cardiff University	Vocational component of the three-step pathway
City Law School, City, University of London	Vocational component of the three-step pathway Vocational component of the four-step pathway (delivered in two parts)
University of Hertfordshire	Vocational component of the three-step pathway Vocational component of the four-step pathway (delivered in two parts)
Inns of Court College of Advocacy	Vocational component of the four-step pathway (delivered in two parts)
University of Law	Vocational component of the three-step pathway
Manchester Metropolitan University	Vocational component of the three-step pathway
Northumbria University	Vocational component of the three-step pathway Vocational component of the four-step pathway (delivered in two parts) Vocational and academic components of the integrated pathway
Nottingham Trent University	Vocational component of the three-step pathway
University of the West of England	Vocational component of the three-step pathway Vocational component of the four-step pathway (delivered in two parts)

Table 4: Bar training provided by AETOs

Bar Professional Training Course

To become a barrister entitled to practise, the Bar Council requires you to take the one-year (full-time) or two-year (part-time) Bar Professional Training Course (BPTC), previously known as the Bar Vocational Course (BVC). A partial distance learning course is also available. Before registering on the BPTC you will need to be admitted to one of the four Inns of Court: Gray's Inn, Inner Temple, Lincoln's Inn, or Middle Temple (all based in central London). These Inns provide support for barristers and student members, advocacy training and other continuing professional development opportunities, lunching and dining facilities and access to common rooms and gardens. The Inns are also responsible for Calling barristers to the Bar, which is the mechanism by which students become barristers once they have completed the BPTC and pupillage (see below).

The BPTC aims to help you gain the knowledge of procedure and evidence and skills of advocacy, conference skills, drafting, legal research, negotiation and opinion writing to prepare you for the practical stage of training on the job, the one year of pupillage. The BPTC is available at 14 different teaching institutions in 22 locations across the country:

- University of Birmingham
- BPP University (Birmingham, Bristol, Leeds, London and Manchester)
- University of Bristol
- Cardiff Law School
- City Law School
- Inns of Court College of Advocacy
- The University of Law (Birmingham, Leeds, London, Manchester and Nottingham)
- University of Leeds
- University of London
- University of Manchester
- Manchester Metropolitan University
- University of Northumbria, Newcastle.
- Nottingham Law School, Nottingham Trent University
- University of the West of England, Bristol

The BPTC costs between £14,000 and £19,400 depending on the chosen institution. Applications must be made directly to the institutions.

Bar Course Aptitude Test (BCAT)

Until recently (31 July 2022), the Bar Standards Board required applicants for the BPTC to pass the Bar Course Aptitude Test (BCAT) before their offer of a place on the BPTC could be confirmed. The purpose of the BCAT was to test applicants' critical thinking and reasoning, which are considered to be the core skills required for the BPTC. The idea was to make sure that students starting the BPTC had the necessary skills to pass it. It is still worthwhile for students to take it in their own time though, as it is a good barometer for them.

The test comprises 60 multiple-choice questions that must be completed in 55 minutes. The test is computerised and must be sat at a Pearson VUE centre. The fee for taking the test is £150 if it is taken in UK and EU test centres and £170 for non-EU test centres.

BCAT registration tends to open in February, with the deadline for booking and completing the exam in September, but early sittings are advised as retake examinations are permitted if the scores required are not obtained.

For more information on the BCAT, including a practice test so that you can familiarise yourself with the type of questions asked, visit www.talentlens.com/uk/about/the-bar-course-aptitude-test-bcat.html.

Pupillage

Pupillage is the final stage to qualifying as a barrister and is hard work. The first six months of pupillage (known as the 'first six') are non-practising and involve training with a senior barrister (your 'pupil supervisor') at work for six months. During the first six months you will be expected to undertake legal research, draft opinions, and read your pupil supervisor's paperwork.

Once you have completed the first six months, you will spend the second six months (the 'second six') practising and be able to appear in court as an advocate. This is when you start to build your own reputation and have your own cases. Pupils must be paid a minimum salary of £17,152 per annum (or £19,144 in London), plus reasonable travel expenses where applicable.

Those of you eager to become a barrister are in for a tough time. Competition for places is very high. The Bar Standards Board website even includes a health warning about the intense competition for pupillages. In 2022, it reported that 2,172 students enrolled on the bar course, whereas the number of pupillages was only 488. To make things even tougher, students are allowed to try to find a pupillage for up to five years after completing the bar course, so in any one year, there could be over 3,000 people applying for pupillages. Some barristers' chambers report having over a hundred applicants for each pupillage placement. Even if you are successful in obtaining a pupillage, there is no guarantee of work after completing it – in every year, there are usually fewer tenancies available at chambers than there are students completing their pupillages, and the opportunities for employed barristers are few and far between. The Bar Standards Board recommends undertaking thorough research to find out if a career at the Bar is really for you, and this includes making a realistic assessment of whether you have the capacity to become a good barrister.

| Student enrolments on BPTC in 2021/2022 | 2,172 |
| Pupillages available in 2021/2022 | 488 |

Table 5: Competition for barristers' pupillages

Applications for pupillage are made through an online pupillage application system, called 'Pupillage Gateway', which is operated by the Bar Council. The system allows applicants to search and apply for pupillage vacancies. All pupillage providers must advertise all pupillage vacancies on the Gateway. There is a common timetable for the application process, which is typically as follows:

- November: Gateway pupillages are listed for browsing and a practice application form becomes available
- January: submission window opens

Getting into Law

- February: submission window closes
- February to April: interview period
- May: offers made.

No charge is made to applicants. For more information and specific dates for the application process for a particular year, visit www.pupillagegateway.com.

Before applying, you should find out as much as possible about your preferred set of chambers. You should study the chambers' website carefully and look at online bar directories. You should also try to attend a pupillage fair. These are held every so often to enable students who wish to pursue a career at the Bar to meet different sets of chambers.

Case study

Rob is a well-established barrister with over 20 years' experience in a wide range of areas, encompassing international, immigration, public and serious fraud law. His expertise in human rights has gained him several visiting lectureships.

'A huge part of being a barrister is just being approachable, being able to think hard and consistently, and having a very strong work ethic. All of those elements are required for success as a barrister. It's a challenging role, and there are times when your work-life balance suffers as a consequence of the workload. It's certainly never boring! You have to work hard to keep up to date with the law, which is my favourite aspect of being a barrister – the constant challenge and learning – though at times it can be exhausting!

'When I embarked on my pupillage, I rotated through various areas on mini pupillages to narrow down the areas that I was interested in pursuing. I now focus on extradition, immigration and international crime. This means I have to stay up to date on other countries' legal systems to do the best work for my clients. Recently, Brexit has caused significant ripples in the legal system, and it has been very interesting working in immigration in this context.

'Before pursuing law, I studied economics with history at university, and qualified as a barrister following the completion of the law conversion course (PGDL), then the Bar vocational course. After completing the academic qualifications, I worked as a paralegal for a year to gain experience in a legal setting before starting work as a barrister the following year. Getting a pupillage was difficult, even back then, which is why the year of work was invaluable, but in today's climate, it is even more so. My advice to aspiring lawyers would be to take every opportunity of experience that presents

> itself, as it might just be that extra something that sets you apart from everyone else.
>
> 'As well as working as a barrister, I also deliver lectures on human rights in a UK university, and I try to incorporate as many of my own cases as possible to illustrate these. Of course, it adds to the workload, but lecturing is also a very nice privilege for those deemed experts in a field.'

Funding your qualification

The average cost of completing the vocational stage of training can surpass £20,000 if living expenses are taken into account. The fees for the BPTC for 2023/2024 were between £12,200 and £18,350 for the year. Scholarships, grants and awards for Bar training are limited, with some provided by the Inns of Court and certain chambers. The majority of students have to depend on bank loans or other financial support. For more information, please visit the individual chambers' websites or consult the Bar Council website.

Advocates: Scotland

The academic and vocational stages are the same as qualifying as a solicitor in Scotland (see the section on qualifying as a solicitor in Scotland on page 69. The intending advocate in Scotland needs to take a law degree followed by the postgraduate Diploma in Professional Legal Practice plus a minimum of 21 months' training in a Scottish solicitor's office.

This is followed by nine months' further unpaid practical training called 'devilling', or work-shadowing. Initially, this involves a Foundation course where the pupils' oral and written advocacy skills are developed through intensive workshops and seminars. There are further compulsory skills courses that must be completed. Pupils will also work for an experienced advocate who has been practising for more than seven years (a 'devilmaster'), to gain experience of civil practice and the criminal courts. Passing the Diploma in Professional Legal Practice culminates in the completion of the Faculty of Advocates' written examinations. The Faculty does not charge for the training and scholarships are available to support with living costs.

Please visit the Faculty of Advocates website for more information: www.advocates.org.uk/about-advocates/becoming-an-advocate.

Barristers: Northern Ireland

Details on how to qualify as a barrister in Northern Ireland are available on the website of the Bar of Northern Ireland (www.barofni.com/page/becoming-a-barrister). The academic stage is the same as for qualifying as a solicitor; students must have completed a recognised law degree (see page 72). For the vocational stage of training, students must complete the one year full-time Bar Postgraduate Diploma in Professional Legal Studies at the Institute of Professional Legal Studies, Queen's University Belfast (the IPLS). After graduating from the Institute when they have passed the Bar course, students are called to the Bar of Northern Ireland. Bar trainees must then undertake a pupillage with a master for a period of 12 months.

Case study

Niall works as a self-employed barrister in Northern Ireland, and is a visiting lecturer at several universities.

'I had visions of working in accounting and finance as a youngster, and for this reason I studied finance at Queen's University Belfast for my undergraduate degree. After graduating, I started to work in an accounting firm, but was more drawn to the legal proceedings. After talking to the legal team there and shadowing some of their work, I decided to study a law conversion course with BPP Law School and immediately followed this up with the Postgraduate Diploma in Professional Legal Studies (Bar).

'The academic training component for law was very rigorous, with lots of reading and cases to work through. For the most part, I found the work very interesting, but there were also some incredibly dull elements. When studying law, don't be put off if you find some areas dull – you will naturally find yourself more drawn to some areas and you can pursue those. I especially enjoyed constitutional and public law, which are the areas I focus on in my work now, both as a lawyer and a lecturer. After being called to the Bar, I undertook a 12-month pupillage. This was a steep learning curve, but I enjoyed being able to put everything into practice and seeing it in action. Taking my own cases was daunting at first, but thorough preparation is key to settling the nerves.'

'The best way to get a bad law repealed is to enforce it strictly.'

Abraham Lincoln

5 | Due process: Getting work experience

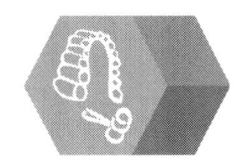

Getting work experience is crucial in terms of helping you secure a training contract or pupillage in today's extremely competitive climate. It is not enough to be purely a brilliant academic. The more relevant experience you have, the better the chance of succeeding.

You can apply for work experience at any stage in the qualification process, whether it be during A levels, during a law (or other) degree, or even at a later stage if you are having trouble obtaining a training contract or pupillage. There are many types of vacation schemes run by the larger firms of solicitors, and chambers also offer mini pupillages; these are invaluable ways of gaining experience and getting a foot in the door. You will be much more attractive to potential employers if you can show that you have relevant work experience. Most of these work experience schemes are only available to undergraduates.

However, having some work experience is also very useful in applying to university for a law degree. You are less likely to be able to find a place on a formal work experience programme while you are still at school, but you should still look for some sort of experience just to get you into a legal environment and see what lawyers actually do. This will support your application for a law degree and help you write the personal statement on your UCAS form. Most importantly, though, it will allow you to see whether a career in law is really for you.

What can you gain from work experience?

When considering a career in any field, work experience is an excellent way of gaining an invaluable insight into the profession. Work placements within a legal setting will enable you to see whether a career in law is for you. You should endeavour to organise placements in the specific field of law in which you are interested. If you are unsure, try and obtain experience in various settings to enhance your knowledge of the different areas within the legal field. Work experience would be beneficial for a number of reasons, including the following.

- It will give you a real insight into the profession. You will be able to observe the day-to-day duties of legal professionals and identify the skills that their roles command. It will also give you an excellent opportunity to weigh up the pros and cons of becoming a lawyer. This can be further explored by discussing the profession with the individuals that you are working with, as they will be able to give you honest answers to your questions. Finally, you will be able to see whether being a barrister or a solicitor is for you, and if it is the latter, the type of law firm in which you would prefer to work.
- By observing legal professionals in practice and reflecting on their duties, you will be much more informed when discussing your interests and aptitude in your personal statement when applying for a law degree at university, and in your applications for legal jobs. Undertaking these placements will demonstrate your commitment to a career in law, and prove that you have given it some real thought.
- Working with legal professionals will allow you to build those all-important contacts that will be beneficial in an extremely competitive environment. Providing that you are able to demonstrate your enthusiasm and willingness to learn, you should be able to secure some strong references, as well as the possibility of acquiring further placements at a later stage.
- By developing your knowledge of what a particular role entails and getting a feel for the pace and demands of the job, work experience will help you to make the transition into full-time work once you have completed the academic component of qualification.

However, it is not that easy getting legal work experience, and can in itself be a competitive process. Most universities and employers recognise this and do not stipulate that work experience is essential, although it is preferred and you should put some considerable effort into obtaining some. This will allow you to reflect on the skill set commanded and demonstrate that you are conscious of the skills that need to be developed. If you cannot get experience in a firm of solicitors or chambers, any work experience that demonstrates use of the skills they are interested in will be valuable. Skills such as communication, determination and business awareness can all be developed in many other sectors of business and commerce. Even just showing that you can get up every day and present yourself for work at 9 o'clock in the morning is of some use.

There are also other ways of gaining relevant legal experience while you are at school or university, for example, participating in a debating society or in mooting or mock trials will help hone your advocacy skills. Some university students hoping to enter the legal profession volunteer at their university law centre or law clinic.

Generally, universities state that if you are able to undertake work experience, it will undoubtedly benefit your understanding of what the role entails and therefore support your application. However, being unable to do so will not put applicants at a disadvantage. In essence, any way in which you can demonstrate that you have made the effort to develop your understanding of what a career in law involves will be viewed as being beneficial. This could be demonstrated through wider reading, extra-curricular activities and visits to law courts, for example. Academic attainment is the main reason behind offers being made, though if an offer is narrowly missed, a strong overall application based on a competent knowledge of what the course and career entail could allow for some leniency on results day.

Similarly, employers understand that securing mini pupillages or placements on vacation schemes is tough owing to the extremely competitive climate. While it is inevitable that the knowledge and skills obtained on these placements will be invaluable in your development as a lawyer, the same skills can be developed elsewhere, such as mooting experience, voluntary work and alternative work experience placements. Mini pupillages and vacation schemes are designed to be enjoyable and useful, but they are not a prerequisite for securing a pupillage or a training contract.

If you look through the case studies contained in this book, it is noticeable that all the young lawyers did a variety of work experience while at school and university, and they all think it played an important part in landing them a job at the end of their studies.

Things to consider during work experience

Work experience placements provide you with excellent opportunities to cultivate knowledge of the field and an understanding of the career. As a result, it is crucial that you are aware of what is going on around you so that you can develop your insight.

Making a good impression

In general, you should aim to maintain a high level of professionalism throughout the duration of your placement. Remember, the legal professionals that you work with at this point could play a crucial role in the development of your career at a later stage. With this in mind, always try to adopt the following attitudes.

- **Maintain a formal appearance:** dress smartly and present yourself appropriately. If you are unsure of how to dress, it is always better to wear more formal attire.
- **Be polite:** offer to help with routine tasks where sensible and aim to show your interest by asking questions. In general, people will be quite flattered when you show an interest in their role and how they reached that point in their career, so don't be afraid to demonstrate

your curiosity! If you show that you are friendly and reliable, there is a greater chance of you acquiring more opportunities.
- **Be organised:** make sure that you are on time and plan your commute accordingly. Punctuality makes a lasting impression! You should also make sure that you take anything with you that might be required, such as a pen, a notebook and any formal documentation that may have been requested, such as proof of identity. Similarly, make sure that you organise your time effectively so that you can complete set tasks, and note down the times of meetings or hearings that you have been invited to attend.
- **Be enthusiastic:** demonstrate your competence by completing all tasks that you are set, and don't shy away from responsibility. No one is expecting you to get everything right – work experience is a learning curve, so get stuck in! If you think you have something valuable to say, raise it. Regardless of whether your suggestion is taken up, it will give employers a chance to see that you are really interested.

Doing all of these things will get you on the right track for making the most of your work experience placement. It is also worth considering the following aspects.

The qualities possessed by lawyers

Depending on whether a lawyer is practising as a barrister or a solicitor, they will need to possess and consistently exhibit a range of skills that allow them to carry out their roles successfully. During your placement, it is important to keep a keen eye on the characteristics that the lawyer demonstrates when carrying out their everyday duties. Being able to reflect on these qualities will be an important part of your qualification process; in written applications it will show your knowledge about the skills required to excel in the field, and provide useful aspects to discuss at interview. It will also allow you to identify traits that you need to develop yourself.

Day-to-day tasks

A work experience placement will give you a really thorough insight into a typical day for a solicitor or a barrister. Though it can be argued that there is no 'typical day' and tasks can be quite varied, it should give you a strong indication of what is expected. From this, you should be able to determine whether a career as a solicitor or a barrister is for you.

Solicitors tend to work with clients more closely, typically as part of a larger team. As such, solicitors must hone their communication skills to effectively convey legal positions in layman's terms. This contrasts heavily with the independent work of a barrister, who must then present cases in court following instruction from a client or solicitor. Therefore, the daily tasks for each job could differ significantly, and work experience should allow you to see which elements appeal to you and which do not.

The roles of other legal professionals

Through your time in a legal practice, it is important to consider the roles of staff other than solicitors or barristers. For example, legal secretaries, paralegals and legal executives will all work alongside and for solicitors, and it is essential to acquire an understanding of how these individuals work together to form a functional team. Make sure that you take the time to speak to as many people in different roles as possible, showing an interest in the specific tasks that they undertake.

Working as a lawyer

There is no denying that qualifying as a lawyer is tough, with high demands and long hours. It is for this reason that it is so important that you ask questions about these aspects: find out which areas of the job lawyers find rewarding, and which areas they dislike.

Keeping a work experience diary

Your work experience will likely be fundamental when looking to develop your career. With this in mind, it is worth you making notes of any interesting observations so that you have a full record to review in preparation for university applications, job applications and interviews.

It is advisable to lay out a formal diary in which you list your daily activities, noting down any key observations regarding specific tasks that were undertaken by lawyers and the skills that they used to conduct them effectively. Keeping a notebook with you will also allow you to jot down any questions that you may have, as well as the answers given to those questions.

Where to apply for work experience

Law firms' vacation schemes for aspiring solicitors

The big corporate law firms offer a range of different vacation schemes, and if you are at all interested in this type of law, you should apply for some of these while studying law at undergraduate level. If you are interested in commercial law, but do not necessarily want to train at one of the biggest firms, it is still useful to have done one of these vacation schemes as it will impress any smaller commercial firm that you may apply to for a training contract by showing that you have done your research into working as a commercial solicitor. Even if you are not sure what type of law you are really interested in (or, indeed, whether you would like to become a solicitor or barrister) it is worth applying for some of these schemes as it may help you make up your mind.

There are different sorts of schemes depending on what stage of your education you are at and whether or not you are studying law at university. Many firms offer shorter 'taster' schemes for first year undergraduates, followed by slightly longer schemes (of two, three or four weeks) for students in their penultimate year of university. The same schemes may be open to those taking a non-law degree, or different schemes may be available. Most take place during the summer, but some are available during other university holiday periods. To research these vacation schemes, you need to look at the websites of all the big law firms. There are often strict application timetables that require you to apply up to a year in advance (so, for example, in the first term of the academic year for a placement the following summer).

Generally, vacation schemes pay a small amount of money to cover your expenses while you are there. Many of these big firms link their vacation schemes to their training contracts. You may not necessarily have to do a vacation scheme to be offered a training contract, but it will certainly help, and some firms use vacation schemes as a way of finding suitable candidates to offer training contracts to. Some firms recruit trainees almost exclusively from their vacation schemes. They will also give you a genuine insight into the culture of the different firms and help you decide where you would like to work. One junior solicitor commented that she only applied to firms that she had done a vacation scheme with as she knew much more about what they were like and whether she would enjoy working there.

Mini pupillages at chambers

Similarly, many barristers' chambers offer mini pupillages, which allow you to shadow a practising barrister for up to two weeks to find out what working as a barrister is really like. If you think that there is any possibility that you might like to become a barrister, then it is crucial to try hard to undertake a mini pupillage. You can search online for barristers' chambers that offer mini pupillages and there are also online search tools available, such as at www.lawcareers.net.

'Informal' placements

Work experience can also take place on less of a formal basis than a vacation scheme or mini pupillage through shadowing court officers or a barristers' clerk. Such work experience would be invaluable for a university application.

As vacation schemes are incredibly competitive and only offered by a small subset of practices, you can take a speculative approach to applying by contacting law firms directly. This could involve a phone call, email or face-to-face discussion initially, but is usually followed up by sending in a CV and covering letter for consideration. An excellent time to procure such placements would be during summer and Easter breaks. Both the Law Society and the Legal 500 list UK law firms with contact details and provide a useful source of information when making speculative applications.

In the same way, you can also approach sets of chambers that do not offer formal mini pupillage schemes. The Chambers and Partners directory provides the names and addresses of UK chambers.

Voluntary work

Some legal work can be undertaken on a voluntary basis and, for several reasons, conducting such work would prove to be invaluable in terms of developing the necessary skills to succeed in the field of law.

Perhaps the most useful voluntary work that can be undertaken to enhance your legal skills is voluntary work at a law clinic, which is accessible to undergraduate students. A variety of roles can be undertaken, and all of these will allow you to witness first-hand the range of queries that arise and the manner in which they are dealt.

The Citizens Advice Bureau and the Free Representation Unit also provide volunteer opportunities with a legal basis, giving you the opportunity to gain experience in dealing with several legal issues such as housing and welfare law. It will also allow you to develop your understanding of how to appropriately advise clients.

However, voluntary work does not necessarily have to have a legal basis for it to be useful. Volunteer work in any field presents a wide range of opportunities to engage with people from different backgrounds and age groups, and gain new or develop existing skills as well as confidence. Maintaining a long-term voluntary position demonstrates an individual's commitment to helping society and developing their skills in communication. It will also give you the chance to enhance your understanding of the wider world.

As most charitable organisations are enthusiastic about recruiting volunteers, securing a placement should not be too difficult. Examples of areas that could be considered include:

- **charity work:** typically involves working in a charity shop or supporting the fundraising efforts of a charitable organisation
- **care work:** provides the opportunity to develop your communication skills when working with vulnerable people
- **humanitarian work:** will improve your understanding of wider international issues, potentially presenting you with the opportunity to overcome obstacles in communication such as language barriers
- **educational work:** supporting students in schools or voluntary teaching roles, e.g. teaching English to refugees.

Information on voluntary positions can be found on a number of websites, including:

- Do-It (https://do-it.life)
- Volunteering Matters (https://volunteeringmatters.org.uk)
- NCVO (www.ncvo.org.uk/ncvo-volunteering/i-want-to-volunteer)
- Volunteer Scotland (www.volunteerscotland.net)
- Volunteer Wales (www.volunteering-wales.net).

Other potential sources of useful experience

Outside of work experience and voluntary placements, additional valuable experience could be obtained elsewhere.

- Internships within the legal sector, which typically last several months and take place during the summer holidays.
- Joining an Inn provides opportunities in mentorship, marshalling with a judge (i.e. shadowing and sitting with a judge in court), and in-house societies for aspiring barristers.
- Extra-curricular activities, such as involvement in law societies at university, participating in debating societies and mooting competitions. Similarly, joining finance-related societies could prove to be beneficial if you are considering a career in the commercial sector.
- Courts allow the public to observe lawyers in action, making this an easy way to observe court activity.

Looking through the case studies (and example personal statements) contained in this book will also give you some ideas.

Try as many ways of getting work experience as you can think of and be creative in the process. Here are a few suggestions.

- Ask your teachers at school/college if they have any contacts in the legal profession.
- Use your careers service and speak to your careers officer.
- Talk to your family and friends and ask them if they can suggest anyone to contact.
- Make sure everyone you know is aware you are looking for work experience.
- You can also approach sets of chambers that do not offer formal mini pupillage schemes. The Chambers and Partners directory will also give you names and addresses of chambers.

While you are trying to get work experience, you should make sure that you keep up to date with current affairs relating to the legal world and the legal profession by reading a quality newspaper and looking at specialist journals such as *The Law Society Gazette* and *The Lawyer*, which should both be available from large public libraries and are also online (see Chapter 12, page 166 for details).

You should ask to go in for one or two weeks' work experience during the holidays or even just ask for one day's work-shadowing to get an insight into what the working environment is like. Anything that anyone is prepared to give you will be useful. Whichever route you take will almost certainly be unpaid unless you have specific skills to offer, such as good office and keyboard skills. If you can touch-type, you could try to get some paid work with a firm of solicitors during the summer or register with an employment agency.

Virtual Work Experience

Since the Covid-19 pandemic, online or 'virtual' work experience opportunities have become readily accessible and widely acknowledged by universities. These virtual placements can give you an excellent insight into what the career entails, and will highlight to admissions tutors that you are well-informed about the study and practice of law. It should also help you to decide whether it is an area you definitely want to pursue.

Online work experience opportunities

There are many virtual work experience opportunities, most of which can be accessed via the job simulation website www.theforage.com or the companies' own websites.

- Allen & Overy: two 4–6-hour programmes, one in technology/mergers and acquisitions law and one in employment law
- Bird & Bird: content includes 6–8 hours of firm-specific work situations, commercial awareness development and document review/drafting/analysis
- Bright Network Internship Experience: offers sessions on commercial law suitable for A level students, undergraduate students and graduates
- Clifford Chance Virtual Internship: offers a number of self-paced virtual internships covering business and human rights, climate change and cyber security
- Clyde & Co: offers 6–6.5 hours covering a range of topics, including climate change, intellectual property and real estate
- Herbert Smith Freehills: multiple programmes covering digital law, financial services regulation and global litigation, and providing a great range of practice area insights
- Hogan Lovells: branded as the 'UK Virtual Programme' within their BaSE programme (emphasis on diversity); content includes a range of issues, including disputes, mergers, etc.
- Latham & Watkins: offer a huge number of programmes in varied practice areas – mergers and acquisitions, white collar investigations, emerging companies, intellectual property litigation,

Getting into Law

> restructuring, banking and antitrust/competition – providing an exceptional range of practice area insights
> - Pinsent Masons Virtual Work Experience: an online platform that allows aspiring solicitors to see behind the scenes at the firm, assist with helping a hypothetical client and gain practical skills. As it is quite a challenging course, it is targeted at degree-level students, but may also be useful for A level students considering their options
> - Slaughter and May: a 5–6-hour programme of a wide range of tasks, including Requests for Proposals, business development, etc.

As well as online work experience placements, there are a variety of online courses, sometimes known as MOOCs (massive open online courses), that may also be valuable in improving your knowledge of law and developing your applications. The FutureLearn platform is an excellent, free resource with hundreds of law-related courses that are led by leading universities. These range from introducing law as an area of undergraduate study to detailed reviews of specific areas of law, such as human rights and commercial law.

Some courses that may be of particular interest to aspiring lawyers include:

- Exploring Law: Studying Law at University – University of Cambridge (www.futurelearn.com/courses/exploring-law-studying-law-at-university)
- Introduction to Studying Law – The University of Law (www.futurelearn.com/courses/international-foundation-programme-in-law-the-first-step-towards-your-future-successful-career)
- How to Become a Lawyer – The University of Law (www.futurelearn.com/courses/how-do-i-become-a-lawyer).

Additional law-related courses can be found on the Law Courses section on the FutureLearn website (www.futurelearn.com/subjects/law-courses).

How to apply

CV

Many formal vacation schemes and mini pupillages will require you to apply online using an application form. For anything else, you will probably need to put together a CV to support your application. This is a summary of what you have done in your life to date. If you have hardly any work experience then one page on good-quality A4 paper will be sufficient. If you are a mature student with a lot of jobs behind you there is sometimes a case for going on to a second page. So what should go into your CV? Here are the main headings:

- name
- contact details
- education and qualifications
- previous work experience.

There is no standard CV but there is a sample on page 94. Make sure to include the following points. You should ensure that you don't leave any gaps and account for all your time. Also, if something such as illness prevented you from reaching your potential in your exams, point this out in the covering letter (see page 95). Lawyers have excellent attention to detail, so make sure your spelling and grammar are perfect!

Education

Start with your present school, college or university and work back to the beginning of secondary school. No primary schools please! List the qualifications with grades you already have and the ones you intend to sit.

Work experience

Start with the most recent. Don't worry if you've only had a Saturday job at the local shop or a paper round. Put it all down and focus on drawing out any relevant skills that you have gained from it. Employers like to see that you are able to carefully consider your experiences.

Skills

List those such as computer skills, software packages used, languages and driving licence.

Interests and positions of responsibility

What do you like to do in your spare time? If you are or have been captain of a sports team, been a committee member or even head boy or head girl at school, put it all down.

Referees

Usually two: an academic referee such as a teacher or head of your school plus someone who knows you well personally, who is not a relative, such as someone for whom you have worked.

A sample CV

PERSONAL DETAILS
Patrick Jones
17 Bloomsbury Road
Leeds LS1 1XJ
01234 567890
patrickjones@btinternet.com

EDUCATION & QUALIFICATIONS
2023–present: Law LLB, University of Leeds
Year 1 Modules included Foundations in Law, Contract Law, Constitutional Law and Criminal Law
2015–2022: Leeds High School
A levels: Government & Politics (A), Biology (A), Physics (A)
GCSEs: English Language (A*/8), English Literature (A/7), Maths (A*/8), Geography (A/7), German (A/7), Latin (A*/8), Physical Education (B/6), Science (B/6), Additional Science (B/6)

WORK EXPERIENCE
Citizens Advice Bureau, September 2023–present: Shadowing legal volunteers providing advice regarding employment law to develop my knowledge of the cases requiring legal support and assisting with legal research and drafting.
Leeds Tuition Centre, July 2022–present: Paid role tutoring young people in maths and English, which has allowed me to develop my skills in communication and build my confidence in a person-centred role.
Call Centre Operative, February 2020–July 2022: Providing customer support by using my initiative to handle complaints for a commercial company while developing my skills in verbal and written communication.

SKILLS
Computing: competent in Microsoft Word, Excel and PowerPoint.

POSITIONS OF RESPONSIBILITY
Secretary of the University of Leeds Law Society: Organising memberships, handling law society emails and acting as the interface between the society and its members.

INTERESTS
Rugby and Spanish.

REFERENCES

Mrs B Greene	Mr A Jones
Personal Tutor at University of Leeds	Legal Volunteer at Leeds
b.a.greene@leeds.ac.uk	Citizens Advice Bureau
	a.jones@cab.org

Covering letter

Every CV or application form should always be accompanied by a covering letter. The letter is important because it is usually the first thing a potential employer reads.

Here are some tips.

- The letter should be on the same A4 plain paper as your CV and should look like a professional document. It should be no longer than one side of A4.
- Employers accept typed letters, unless they specifically request one to be handwritten.
- Find out the name of the person to whom you should send your letter and CV. It makes a great difference to the reader if you can personalise your application. If you start the letter 'Dear Mr Brown', remember you should finish it 'Yours sincerely'.
- The first paragraph should tell the reader why you are contacting them and what stage of your education you are at.
- The second paragraph should give them some brief information to make them interested in you, e.g. highlighting your interest in law, along with some specific IT skills.
- Thirdly, explain why you are applying to them, for example interest in their line of work, desire to experience work in a small/large firm/set, etc. Mention anything you already know about the firm/chambers and make sure that it is correct. Look carefully at their website and make sure you know what area of the law they practise in!
- Check very carefully for spelling and grammatical mistakes.

A sample covering letter is shown below.

Dear Mr Cooper,

I am an aspiring solicitor currently in my second year of the undergraduate law course at the University of Leeds. In order to enhance my exposure to legal work and learn more about the profession, I am interested in securing a work experience placement, and wondered whether SPM LLP would have any opportunities available.

I am extremely interested in the field of land law, and can see from your website that SPM LLP has an outstanding reputation in this area both nationally and internationally.

I am currently undertaking an independent research project under supervision into this field, in preparation for the upcoming land law module on the course, which has cemented my interest in this area. I have volunteered alongside trained solicitors at the Citizens Advice Bureau to develop my insight into legal work and to

Getting into Law

> practise the skills required, such as research and both written and verbal communication.
>
> Please do not hesitate to contact me if you require any further information or would like to meet me in person.
>
> Yours sincerely,
>
> Patrick Jones

> **Case study**
>
> Alesha is currently in her third year of a law degree at the University of Warwick.
>
> 'Prior to starting my law degree, I had not obtained any legal work experience as it is difficult to obtain. However, I had always been interested in law as an academic subject and learning about its operation in society. Attending the Crown Court and sitting in on cases allowed me to explore my interest and helped me to decide that it was a career that I could really see myself following in the future. I also attended lectures given by barristers and scholars of law. While providing a great opportunity to learn more about my chosen field, this was also a really good way to network and speak to legal professionals, which allowed me to learn about the way that law is practised and implemented.
>
> 'I studied humanities-based subjects at A level, including English literature, politics, history and classics. These provided a really good foundation for developing my essay writing skills and prepared me for the vast amount of reading required for studying law at undergraduate level! Getting the A level grades required is by far the most important aspect of your application, especially when aiming to secure a place at a top university, and this will also impact your employability later in life. I would advise getting involved with extra-curricular activities such as debating, as this will help to make your application stand out and provide examples where you can demonstrate your advocacy skills.
>
> 'When trying to identify the right university for you, it is important to look at the modules taught in each of the years and its assessment methods. At Warwick, I have really enjoyed learning about how law relates directly to society as a whole. Global intellectual property law and international law have been the modules that I have found the most interesting and are the fields that I am considering as a career. It is also well worth investigating the

department's links to solicitors' firms and chambers, as these will be crucial in helping you secure placements and experience in the future.

'Most universities will provide law-specific societies and I would encourage getting involved as much as possible, as applying for graduate positions is extremely competitive so you will need to stand out! I have been involved in a number of activities, including:

- participating in first year CMS mooting competition
- participating in Warwick witness examination competition
- attending a "Day in the City" event which involved visiting Chambers in London and the Royal Courts of Justice
- getting involved with societies and becoming Vice President of the Warwick Bar Society for aspiring barristers (where I was also able to develop important skills in organising the Law Ball)
- an internship at the Houses of Parliament
- participating in an international venture – Warwick Finance Societies in Dubai
- attending insight days at Dubai Islamic Bank, PwC, The Boston Consulting Group, AL Tamimi & Company, Freshfields Bruckhaus Deringer, Linklaters, Francis Taylor Building and Quadrant Chambers
- mini pupillages at St Ives Chambers and 2 Bedford Row
- being Campus Representative for The University of Law.

'Undertaking all of these additional elements has been time consuming, and some of them have been difficult to secure, but they have been invaluable in allowing me to learn new skills, gain hands-on experience that I can use to demonstrate those skills and identify what exactly I want to pursue as a career.

'I hope to become a barrister following graduation. At the moment, I am applying for the BPTC and trying to secure funding through an Inns of Court Scholarship. I will then undertake a pupillage as a training year before eventually being called to the Bar.'

Derived from the Latin for 'twist', what term is used in common law for a civil wrong that causes a party loss or harm?

Answer: Tort

6 | Conveyancing: Choosing your law degree

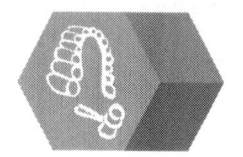

This chapter focuses on how to go about choosing a law degree. The aim is to produce a shortlist of degree courses you are interested in and from that to choose the top five courses to put down in your UCAS application.

As previous chapters have made clear, you do not need a law degree to enter the legal profession. Equally, a law degree can be an excellent springboard into a wide range of other careers. Employers are generally impressed by a good-calibre law graduate, since law is known to be a challenging discipline requiring skills such as research, analysis, application, clarity, advocacy and effective written communication. These are relevant in many other careers as well as those in the legal professions.

If you do not wish to read law at university, most of the advice in this chapter will still be relevant to choosing your degree course, but for more general advice on choosing degree courses, please refer to some of the guides mentioned in Chapter 12.

Things to consider

The basic criteria for choosing your degree course are:

- the type of law course you are interested in
- your academic ability
- where you want to study.

Most of the information you need to know about universities and the courses available at them is available online either through:

- UCAS (www.ucas.com)
- universities' own websites. Most universities have their prospectuses available to download online (although you can request a paper copy to be sent through the post if you prefer) and there should also be information on whom to contact if you have a specific question.
- university comparison guides and league tables such as the Complete University Guide (www.thecompleteuniversityguide.co.uk) and the Guardian University Guide (www.theguardian.com/

education/ng-interactive/2023/sep/09/the-guardian-university-guide-2024-the-rankings). There are also books providing similar information, such as *The Times and Sunday Times Good University Guide*. Make sure you use the most up-to-date edition.

Going to university is an investment, particularly with the rise in tuition fees in recent years, so the choice of what to study and where to apply to must be given careful thought. You will also spend three years of your life there, so you will want to make sure that you will be somewhere you will enjoy living. There are many institutions offering law courses and you will need to look at ways of narrowing down your options.

Types of law degree

Many law degree courses are offered by many different institutions across the country and the choice may at first appear daunting. However, the range of options can quickly be narrowed down once you know what you are looking for. The important thing is to choose the right course for you. The key points to consider are:

- if you intend to qualify as a solicitor or a barrister in the future, the degree must be a qualifying law degree (QLD); if you want to be a solicitor, you will need to take take the SQE, and if you wish to become a barrister, you need to complete the BPTC
- whether you should choose an LLB or a BA (and whether it matters)
- should you choose a single or joint honours degree?

Note on qualifying law degrees

Qualifying law degrees (QLDs) were recognised by the Solicitors Regulation Authority (SRA) up until September 2021, when the new qualification route for solicitors began. Having a QLD means that you have studied the subjects which the SRA consider to be the core foundation subjects for any lawyer, including criminal law, equity and the law of trusts, law of the European Union, obligations (including contract, restitution and tort law), property law and public law (including constitutional law, administrative law and human rights law). These are areas that must be studied in order to commence the LPC, and so the QLD description is likely to remain throughout the transitional period for the new route of qualification.

LLB or BA?

Some law degrees are classified as LLBs, whereas others are BAs. As a broad generalisation, LLB degrees will involve spending all of your time studying law, whereas a BA or BSc degree may involve spending some time studying non-law modules. For historical reasons, the universities of Oxford and Cambridge do not award LLBs at all and their law degrees are BAs. If you are interested in studying non-law modules as part of your law degree (for example, foreign languages), then the increased breadth of a BA of BSc degree may well be preferable for you and also welcomed by future employers.

Single or joint honours?

Law can be taken on its own (a single honours degree) or mixed with one or more other subjects (a joint honours degree).

A single honours degree will allow you to focus on studying law, although some courses will also permit you to take individual modules from other subject areas, even from completely different disciplines. As well as the core subjects, you will also be able to choose optional subjects (particularly in second and later years). Some institutions can offer only a limited selection of options, while others provide a much greater variety. If there is a particular area of law you are interested in, for example intellectual property law, then you may want to apply to a university that offers this as an option.

A joint honours degree will allow you to divide your time between law and one or more other disciplines. Usually, where two subjects in a degree title are joined by the word 'and', this indicates that the course will involve a 50/50 split between the two subjects, whereas the word 'with' suggest a two-thirds/one-third split. However, this is a broad generalisation and you should always check the details of any particular course on the university's website. A popular combination is to study law with a European language, although you should note that these courses often specify that candidates must have an A level or at the very least a GCSE in the relevant language.

Approaches to teaching law

It is interesting to note that there are broadly three different approaches to teaching law, but you should not base your selection on this criterion since few institutions adhere to one kind. Most places are likely to opt for a mixture (sometimes even within an individual unit, especially if it is taught by several different tutors). However, the emphasis of different law schools may be different. The approaches are as follows.

- *Pure academic approach.* This approach focuses on the core legal subjects and doesn't look much beyond statutes and law reports for its sources of law. It provides a thorough grounding in the relevant legal system and its laws.
- *Contextual approach.* Law can also be examined in context; that is to say, law, its role and its effectiveness are looked at in relation to society (past and present), politics and the economy. This approach may include elements of critical legal theory. Students are expected

to analyse the problems (for example, loopholes, contradictions, injustices and so on) within the law. This can make for some heated and controversial seminars.
- *Vocational approach.* This stresses professional training and skills such as negotiating, interviewing, counselling, drafting, research, analysis, clear expression and the ability to read through vast amounts of material, sift out the legally relevant points and present a logical argument. These skills are mainly covered during the vocational stage of training to become a solicitor or barrister, but may also be looked at in a law degree. Extra-curricular activities such as mooting (a mock courtroom trial), debating and law clinics, in which students get the opportunity to help out with a real-life case from start to finish, also help develop these skills at university.

Academic requirements

Entry requirements for law degrees vary greatly, both in terms of the standard that they expect students to have achieved and also in how they are expressed. You will need to research which degrees at which universities your likely A levels, Scottish Highers, IB or BTEC qualifications will enable you to access. It is important to be realistic about the grades you are likely to achieve: don't be too pessimistic, but make sure that the entry requirements for the courses you choose include some safer options. Talk to your teachers for an accurate picture of your predicted results as this will allow you to target universities accordingly. Don't forget that you need to select one or two universities with lower grade requirements than your predictions as 'insurance' choices.

Most of the top universities require applicants to have three A levels (or their equivalent) and the most selective universities, such as Cambridge, now regularly include an A* grade in their offers. Information on the entry requirements for law degrees at different universities is available through UCAS or the websites of the universities themselves.

Less academically selective universities often express their entry requirements as a target number of UCAS Tariff points. The UCAS Tariff system allocates points to the different qualifications taken by students before they access higher education. It therefore allows students with different qualifications to access the same undergraduate degree courses, and allows universities to compare applicants with different qualifications.

Your A level subject choices may also have a bearing on which universities you can realistically expect to receive an offer from. Few courses specify subjects they want you to have studied (with the exception of most language joint degrees), although qualifications in traditional academic subjects are preferred at the more selective universities and are welcomed everywhere. Some universities won't accept A levels such as General Studies or Critical Thinking. No institutions require A level Law from potential students. You should always check carefully on the websites of all the universities that you are interested in to confirm their specific requirements.

If your predicted A level results (or chosen A level subjects) effectively prevent you from taking a law degree, then it's time for a rethink. If you wanted to take a law degree with a view to entering the profession, then you could opt for the non-law degree entry route instead. Most employers stress that a large number of trainee solicitors and pupil barristers have a non-law degree. Remember that if you read a subject other than law, you will still need a thorough knowledge of law for the SQE, so you may need to consider a postgraduate qualification in law or standalone SQE preparation courses. The disadvantage is that the route might be longer and therefore more expensive (if sponsorship cannot be found).

Choosing a university

Once you have made a realistic assessment of your likely A level grades (or other qualifications) you can think about choosing specific institutions. Remember, university life isn't going to be solely about academic study. It is truly a growing experience – educationally, socially and culturally – and besides, three or four years can really drag if you're not happy outside the lecture theatre. Here is an assortment of factors which might help you to choose where you would like to study. Some of these will be more important to you than others, so you should use the paragraphs below to think carefully about the things that matter most to you.

Warning: different legal systems

If you're hoping to practise law, then you must be sure where you intend to work within the UK (i.e. England or Wales, Scotland or Northern Ireland). Since the legal systems differ throughout the UK, you must qualify in the part of the UK you intend to practise in. If you did subsequently decide to move, then it is usually possible to convert qualifications from a different country (e.g. if you qualified in England but want to practise in Scotland). To work in England or Wales having qualified elsewhere, lawyers will have to undertake the Solicitors Qualifying Examination (SQE). More information can be found by visiting the websites of the Law Societies and Bar Councils for each country, mentioned in Chapter 3. More detail on the differences between the professions in each of the UK countries can be found in Chapters 2 and 3.

Open days

If you get the opportunity, attend the open days for the universities where you are interested in studying. Visit the law departments and talk to former or current students and course lecturers and tutors. Doing so should give you an idea of what life on campus at that particular university is like, and this will allow you to determine whether you would enjoy your time there. If you cannot attend any open days, there are often campus tours available, or you can make an independent visit. Try to go on a taster course for law at any university if possible. This does not need to be a university to which you are actually thinking of applying – even if it is not, it will still give you an idea of what to look for in universities in general and will also give you something to mention in your personal statement.

Virtual open days

Since the coronavirus pandemic, many universities have converted their open days into virtual events that are conducted wholly online. A virtual open day is different to visiting a campus in person, but it is still an excellent opportunity to see what a university has to offer and get an insight into a place where you might choose to study.

As you won't have to factor in travelling to the universities, you can attend more open days than you might have initially intended. This might open up more doors for you in terms of your university options.

Virtual open days have differing formats depending on the university, but typically provide an opportunity to look at virtual tours, attend online webinars and talk to current students, lecturers and admissions officers, allowing you to ask any questions that you might have.

Types of university or college

There are a number of ways of categorising universities and higher education colleges, but there are two broad categorisations by which these institutions are often sorted:

Old or new?

Almost all law degrees are taught by universities and these can be categorised as 'old' or 'new'. A few other colleges of higher education also offer law degrees.

1. 'Old' universities. Traditionally the more academic universities with higher admission requirements. They are well established, with good libraries and research facilities, and are well respected by employers and provide an academically rigorous training.
2. 'New' universities. Pre-1992, most of these were polytechnics or institutes of higher education and these generally still hold true to the original polytechnic doctrine of vocational courses and strong

Getting into Law

ties with industry, typically through placements and work experience. Their approach to teaching law may generally be slightly more vocational in nature. They can still be looked down upon by some employers because of their generally lower academic entry requirements, but many of the new universities have a good name for flexible admissions and learning and modern approaches to their degree teaching. There are also some private universities, such as BPP University, the University of Law and Buckingham University. These universities can offer even greater flexibility in the way your degree course is structured. Some private universities now offer the chance to take a degree that would normally take three years in only two years of full-time study, which can be really helpful if you want to qualify as quickly as possible, and possibly of particular interest to mature or overseas students. You will simply forgo the long holidays usually associated with university degree courses. Private universities tend to be more vocational in their approach. They receive no state funding, so are not subject to the government's cap on tuition fees, but may not necessarily be more expensive, especially if you choose the two-year degree option. Some institutions offer part-time degree courses.
3. Colleges of higher education. Usually specialist institutions and therefore provide good facilities in their chosen fields. They are sometimes affiliated to universities, which means the college buys the right to teach the degree, which the university will award, provided that the course meets the standards set by the university.
4. The Open University, which is a very well-established provider of part-time distance-learning degree courses, offers an LLB degree.

City or campus?

Universities are also often divided into campus or city universities. So, when looking at which university to choose you need to consider whether you would prefer to live on a university campus, surrounded by your fellow students and the university's facilities, or whether you would prefer to be more integrated into town or city life. The choice is slightly more sophisticated than this broad division, since many universities offer something of a mix between these two extremes. For example, there are campuses in the middle of, or right on the edge of, cities or towns. Other campuses are practically surrounded by open fields and the nearest town or city is a bus ride away. Some city universities are largely contained in one area, whereas others are spread throughout the city.

The town or city where the university is based, particularly its size, can also have a big effect on the 'feel' of the place. Some city universities have a largely separate university area, but are close to the centre of a large city, such as Leeds. Others are more integrated into the city, such as Sheffield. Some have a largely self-contained campus, but are still in a big city, such as Nottingham. Universities more often thought of as campus universities may be more likely to be near a smaller town than a big city, such as Lancaster and Warwick.

Other factors to consider

Attractiveness to employers

Few employers will openly admit to giving preference to graduates from particular universities. Most are looking for high-quality degrees as an indication of strong academic ability. But since students with higher A level grades tend to go to the older and more prestigious universities, it is unsurprising that a large proportion of successful lawyers come from these universities. Employers are often so swamped with applications that they use university background as an easy way to filter applicants, reckoning that the better universities will have picked the higher-calibre students and therefore have done part of their job for them. It therefore makes sense to be aware of the reputations of the different universities, which can often be gleaned from their position in the league tables, and factor this into your decision. You must obviously choose to go somewhere that you will enjoy, but since (at least part of) the object of the exercise is to find a good job at the end of your university studies, it is foolhardy to ignore how potential employers will view your degree.

Quality of teaching

This is difficult to establish without the benefit of an open day, and even then you will only have the opportunity to meet one or two of the teaching staff and speak to one or two students. However, league tables of universities for each subject are published by several organisations, such as the *Guardian*, the *Times and Sunday Times* and The Complete University Guide. The *Guardian's* 'The best UK universities 2024 – rankings' for law is available online at www.theguardian.com/education/ng-interactive/2023/sep/09/the-guardian-university-guide-2024-the-rankings and the Complete University Guide 2024 Law league table is at www.thecompleteuniversityguide.co.uk/league-tables/rankings/law. *The Times/Sunday Times Guide* is published annually.

The National Student Survey is conducted each year to get feedback from students who have studied at university, and is more focused on overall student satisfaction. Scores are given for many factors, including the quality of teaching and how good teachers are at providing feedback to students. The results of the survey can be seen online, through www.officeforstudents.org.uk/advice-and-guidance/student-information-and-data/national-student-survey-nss. Since the raising of tuition fees, students have become a lot more interested in issues such as teaching quality and 'contact time' – i.e. how much face-to-face teaching you will actually get, and it makes sense to investigate this as much as you can.

Teaching quality may suffer if seminar or tutorial groups are too large, so try to also compare group sizes for the same courses at different institutions.

Educational facilities

Most universities should have a well-stocked and up-to-date law library. They should also have good-quality IT resources and fast broadband internet connections. More vocational courses might also use mock courtrooms with video and audio equipment. The facilities available will depend on the budget of an institution, and obviously how they choose to spend it. You may want to look at the law department at the university. Is it in the new, shiny, state-of-the-art building or a dilapidated 1960s monstrosity hidden from view? At the end of the day, university is about more than just buildings – academically, the quality of teaching is more important and non-academic factors will also make a big difference to whether or not you enjoy your time there. However, if you are concerned about the environment in which you study, you should investigate the building housing the law department.

Non-academic considerations

- **Finances.** The cost of living differs substantially throughout the UK, so will you be able to reach deeper into your pockets for rent or other fundamentals and entertainment if you are living in a major city or in the south? If you are living in London, you will need particularly deep pockets.
- **Distance from home.** Do you want to get away from your family and friends or stay as close to them as possible? While there can be advantages, financially at least, to living at home if you go to your local university, you may prefer the challenge of looking after yourself and the opportunity to be completely independent. You should also think about whether you want to be able to go home at weekends without spending half a day (or more) on a train.
- **Accommodation.** What sort of accommodation is on offer? Do you want to live on campus or in halls of residence with other students, or in private housing that you may need to organise yourself that could be a considerable distance from college? Most universities provide accommodation for first year students at least, but how far this is from the teaching areas of the university will vary. You may simply be able to roll out of bed and totter next door for your 9am lectures, or you may be looking at a half-hour bus journey in rush hour. Some universities offer accommodation beyond the first year, which will save you having to live in private housing.
- **Catering.** Would you prefer to go somewhere where you can have your meals cooked for you, or are you keen to unleash your inner chef and cater for yourself?
- **Interests.** Will the university allow you to pursue your interests? Are you going to be spending much time in, for example, the sports

centre, the theatre or student bars? How about university societies: is there one that allows you to indulge your existing hobbies or the ones you've always dreamt of trying? Most universities have a huge choice of extra-curricular activities and entertainments and very good facilities. However, you should think about exactly what is provided, the standard of participants and whether all abilities are catered for (are you a county squash player or simply keen to have a go?) and how far the facilities that you will want to use are from the accommodation or teaching areas. Some universities have particular reputations for particular extra-curricular activities – for example, Loughborough for sport.

Studying overseas and work placements

The opportunity to study overseas and/or complete a work placement could also be factors affecting your degree selection. Some universities will allow you to go to an overseas university with which they have an arrangement for one year of your studies. Others will allow you to spend a year in the middle of your degree on a work placement. You do not need to be a linguist to study abroad, since you can study or work overseas in English in, for example, North America, the Netherlands or Malaysia.

Prior to Brexit, the Erasmus scheme allowed students from the UK to undertake placements in the EU and vice versa as part of their studies. The Turing scheme has now replaced Erasmus and it provides funding for students who want to undertake study periods or training internationally. UK universities classed as hosting organisations can send students to non-UK higher education providers or non-UK public or private organisations active in the labour market or in the fields of education and training. The scheme is open to undergraduate students and graduates who have received their degrees within the last 12 months. Opportunities to study or work abroad are an exceptional opportunity to develop new skills, gain exposure to new cultures and enhance your employability. Further information can be found on the Turing Scheme website (www.turing-scheme.org.uk), which also has a detailed programme guide that covers eligibility and funding information.

If you are planning to study law at university, these opportunities may be more limited, as law is a very jurisdiction-specific subject.

Similarly, few law degree courses offer work placements during your degree. You will usually need to arrange this for during university holidays (see Chapter 5, page 83).

What 'S' word refers to law that is passed by a body of legislature? Its name resembles sculptures that commemorate historical figures, but not exactly.

Answer: Statutory

7 | Fine print: The UCAS application and the LNAT

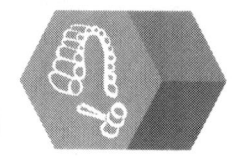

So you have chosen a few universities that you would like to apply to for a law degree; now what? This chapter will guide you through the UCAS application process for a law degree, and then give you some advice if you are applying to any universities that require the LNAT entrance exam.

Suggested application timescale

Below is a suggested timeline that you could follow throughout your time at sixth form or college to ensure that you are thoroughly prepared for your application.

Lower Sixth/Year 12

September–December

- If you already know that you want to study law at university, or you think it could be a serious possibility, the beginning of your A levels is a good time to explore academic options available to you, such as the EPQ if your school or college runs this. Doing so will allow you to start identifying your academic interests within the field of law, and whether or not it might be an area you want to pursue further.

January onwards

- Research degree courses, considering the kind of course you might want to study and where you might want to study.

- Take note of any entry requirements, including GCSE grades, predicted A level grades, and whether or not they require you to sit the LNAT entrance exam.
- Book onto taster courses at universities.
- Discuss your plans with teachers, family and friends, to see whether they have any contacts or insight into the profession.
- Update your CV and start enquiring about work experience placements, writing to any firms or companies that may be able to support you in providing a placement.

April onwards

- Find out when university open days are being held and book onto any of interest to you. A useful tool is www.opendays.com. Always check to see whether the Law department has any specific talks, and book onto them where required to get a good idea of what studying there would be like and to give you the opportunity to ask any questions you might have.

June/July

- Attend any open days that are available and look at university department websites and prospectuses to narrow down your choices.
- Register on UCAS with your school and complete as much of the form as possible with background information and academic exam results to date.

July/August

- Make a shortlist of your courses. Try to do as much research as possible over the summer holidays. This is particularly important for applicants to Oxford and Cambridge.
- Undertake work experience and wider reading (see suggestions in Chapter 12).
- Start writing your personal statement.
- If applicable, review your courses shortlist when you receive your summer exam results.

Upper Sixth/Year 13

September onwards
- Finalise your personal statement and UCAS form, then complete your application and send it off to UCAS.
- Register and book a place to sit the LNAT if you are applying to a university that uses it (see below).

October
- *15 October (6pm UK time):* Deadline for submitting your UCAS application if you are applying for places at Oxford or Cambridge.
- *16 October:* Deadline for sitting the LNAT if you are applying to Oxford or Cambridge. For other universities requiring LNAT, refer to the individual websites for dates.

November
- If you have applied to Oxford or Cambridge, start preparing for the interview stage so that you are ready when the invite arrives!

December
- Interviews for Oxford and Cambridge.

January
- *29 January (6pm UK time):* Deadline for submitting your application to UCAS. While UCAS will process late applications, all universities may not accept them.

February–April

- Decisions (and hopefully, offers!) should arrive during this time. Universities are encouraged to respond by 31 March, but don't worry if you haven't heard back from all of them by this point, especially if your application was late.
- If you have received all your university/college decisions by 31 March, you must tell UCAS which offer you have accepted firmly and which one is your insurance choice by a date yet to be determined by UCAS in May.
- Once you have received decisions from all five of your choices, and were either rejected or have declined the offer you received from all of them, you can enter UCAS Extra, a scheme that allows you to apply to other universities, one at a time. See the UCAS website (www.ucas.com) for details.

May–June

- Sit your exams!

August

- On the third Thursday of August, A level results are available.
- If you got the grades, well done! UCAS will send you confirmation of your place.
- If you missed your grades, don't be too disappointed. Clearing starts straight away so don't waste any time – get hold of a list of unfilled places and contact the universities directly. You will be sent instructions on Clearing automatically.
- UCAS no longer supports students who have performed significantly better than they had expected to approach universities that require higher grades than the offer they were holding; that does not mean you cannot approach universities independently. See Chapter 10 for more information on your options on results day.

The UCAS form

The online UCAS form is accessed through the UCAS website (www.ucas.com). Applicants will need to generate an account on the UCAS Hub. The UCAS Hub is a free tool that allows you to conduct research into your options beyond sixth form and store it all in an accessible way, as well as providing useful resources to help with personal statement and CV writing. While it is encouraged that you utilise the UCAS Hub, as it is an excellent resource that combines all of the information you will need for your application, you can just use it to create an account for your application.

Upon generating an account, you will be asked for the year of entry, the level of study that you are interested in, the country that you are from, your contact preferences and subject areas of interest. These answers will tailor the information presented to you on the UCAS Hub. Most applicants register through their school or college using their buzzword, but it is possible to register independently. Once the account has been created, you can access the UCAS form through the applications section. The application sections are summarised below.

1. **Personal details:** Upon creating an account you will be asked to fill in your personal details, including funding and sponsorship options, residential status, any special needs or disabilities, details of any criminal convictions, and the individual selected as your nominated access (someone who can talk to UCAS on your behalf if required).
2. **Additional information:** This section includes providing information about your ethnic origin, national identity, summer schools and taster sessions that you have attended, care background, parental education and occupational background. This section is used by UCAS to gather information for statistics, so any information you provide here will not be used in the selection process. Only UK applicants are required to fill in this section.
3. **Student finance:** If you are a UK applicant and have selected that you will be using student finance in the personal details section, you can fill in this section. UCAS is not linked to student finance directly, but you can consent to them passing your details on to speed up the application process for getting a loan.
4. **Course choices:** In this section, you can add in up to five university or college choices. If you are applying to Oxford or Cambridge, remember that you can only apply to one of them and you can specify a particular college. If you are applying for deferred entry, you can choose this option here.
5. **Education history:** For this section, you will need to add in any qualifications that you hold with the grade obtained, or with qualifications you are currently studying, the grade must be left as 'pending'.
6. **Employment history:** You can add in the details of up to five paid jobs in this section.

7. **Personal statement:** You will need to write a personal statement that outlines your motivation for studying the course that you have applied for, with a limit of 4,000 characters and 47 lines. This will be reviewed by admissions tutors.
8. **Reference:** Once you have completed your application, click send. If you are applying through your school or college, the application will first be sent to someone who can check your application and provide a reference. If you are applying independently, you will be asked for the details of a referee, who will be contacted by email and asked to upload their details before you are able to send your application to UCAS. Your reference is usually provided by a teacher, or someone who knows your professionally.

> General advice on filling in your UCAS application is given in *How to Complete Your UCAS Application* (Trotman).

Your personal statement

For 2026 entry onwards, it is anticipated that the 4,000-character personal statement will be replaced with six questions:

1. Motivation for this course
2. Preparedness for this course
3. Preparation through other experiences
4. Extenuating circumstances
5. Preparedness for study
6. Preferred learning styles.

This new system is designed to give universities a more focused set of responses to make judgement from. However, at the time of writing, the personal statement is still required, and therefore, we will focus on what you need currently.

The personal statement is the most important part of your UCAS application and is your opportunity to demonstrate that you are fully committed to studying law and have the right motivation and personal qualities to do so successfully. It is therefore vital that you think very carefully about how to complete it so that it shows you in the best possible light. You need to sell yourself to the law admissions tutors. It will take time and effort to get it right, so you must allow yourself plenty of time and not attempt to rush it. Expect to go through many drafts before you come up with the final version that you are happy with.

There will be multiple applicants per place for law degrees. A good personal statement can help you to stand out from the crowd and persuade an admissions tutor to give you an offer rather than one of the other equally well-qualified applicants.

Obviously, there are as many ways of writing a personal statement as there are candidates. There are no rules as such, but you should try and adhere to the following advice.

The personal statement should cover three key areas.

1. Why you want to study the course for which you are applying.
2. Why you would be good at the course and are well qualified to embark on it.
3. What other interests you have and (if possible) what transferable skills they give you which would be relevant for the course.

Section 3 should make up no more than 25% of the personal statement (or even less for the most academically competitive universities, such as Oxford, Cambridge and LSE). The focus should be on your academic interest in the courses applied for, and why you are a good candidate, and in most cases this should account for around 75% of the statement.

Some key points to remember.

- The personal statement must be no longer than 4,000 characters (including spaces). This is a strict limit, so you need to ensure that you do not exceed the character count.
- Write in your own words. The statement must be honest and personal and it must sound like you. After all, it is a *personal* statement, and admissions tutors will be using it to gain an insight into you as a potential student.
- Use evidence. Don't make broad-brush statements, but focus on what you have actually done and what you have learnt from it. Focus on how what you have done has helped you to decide a law degree is for you or to become a good candidate for a law degree.
- Check and re-check the statement for spelling, punctuation and grammar. Even better, ask a parent, teacher or family friend to do this for you.
- Do not over-use superlatives ('most passionate' etc.) although you should sound enthusiastic and committed.

Why you want to study law

The first part of the statement should show why you wish to study for a law degree. You can do this by providing answers to some of the following questions.

- Why do you wish to study law? Money, status or family traditions are not good reasons. Refer to evidence and the things that helped you reach your decision. For example: 'I am particularly interested in pursuing a career at the Bar. My enthusiasm was initially sparked by my active participation in the debating society at school, of which I am president. I found that I thoroughly enjoyed the challenge of putting across my point of view and trying to counteract the opposing argument.'

- What precisely is it about the law that interests you? Give details and examples, referring to recent cases and debates.
- Which particular area of law interests you most and, again, why?
- What related material have you recently read and why did you appreciate it? (See below for further guidance.)
- What legal cases have you followed and what recent judgements have you admired and why?
- What legal controversies have excited you? Are you up to date with current affairs and can you demonstrate your knowledge and understanding?

Well-chosen references to books you have read, including specific information you have gleaned from them, are very helpful. Some suggested reading for aspiring law students is contained in Chapter 12. Be careful not to just reel off a list of books – be specific about what interested you about them and what you learnt from them. You should also refer to any law taster courses you have attended but, again, don't just mention them – spell out what you gained from going to them and how they helped you decide that you would like to study law. You should also refer to any current legal issues appearing in the press and what you think of them or have learnt from them.

Work experience is very useful as it demonstrates a commitment to the subject outside the classroom, so mention any experience, paid or voluntary. Explain concisely what your job entailed and what you got out of the whole experience. Even if you haven't been able to get legal work experience, if you have spoken to anyone in the legal profession about their job, then it is worth mentioning as it all builds up a picture of someone who is keen and has done some research. Wanting to be like the characters in legal dramas on television is not enough, and neither is wanting to follow in a parent's footsteps!

Future plans, if any, should also be included on your form. Do not mention a desire to make a lot of money, since this is unlikely to impress admissions tutors who may well have shunned lucrative career opportunities in order to pursue an academic career.

Why you are a good candidate

You should also set out what makes you a good candidate for a law degree. If you have already explained why you wish to be a lawyer and how you made that decision, you will already have gone a long way towards demonstrating that you will be a committed student of the law. However, you should also briefly explain how your current school subjects (usually A levels) prepare you for studying a law degree. What skills have they allowed you to develop? If you have taken only maths and science A levels, you will need to describe how you are prepared for the more literary aspects of a law degree – i.e. reading and assimilating lots of information and preparing longer pieces of written work. You will also need to show that you can write an essay, so it would be a good idea to discuss any work you have carried out beyond your A levels, such as completion of the EPQ.

Extra-curricular activities and transferable skills

The last part of the statement should set out your extra-curricular activities, with a particular emphasis on what key transferable skills they have given you – for example, teamwork, self-motivation or leadership skills. If possible, you could try to link these in with the skills that will be necessary when studying for a law degree. If you are a school prefect, or team captain, then mention it here.

If you are planning to do so, state your reasons for applying for deferred entry and outline what you intend to do during your gap year. For example, you might be planning to find some relevant work experience in a firm of solicitors, and then spend some time overseas to brush up your language skills.

General advice

It is imperative that the focus of your personal statement be on the course of study that you wish to follow. Make sure that for each point you make, whether that be which A levels you are studying or the work experience that you have done, you are relating it back to the course.

Many universities now publish detailed advice about what they are looking for in a personal statement on their websites. You should carefully check the websites of all the universities you wish to apply to and make sure that you follow their advice. Most of it will simply be along the lines of the advice given above, but you should make sure you address any specific requirements or suggestions from the universities you are particularly interested in. You should also bear in mind the way that the universities describe the courses you are interested in on their websites. For example, if they emphasise the need for a practical approach, then it makes sense to highlight how you demonstrate an ability to be practical.

Finally, you should try to avoid some common pitfalls when writing your statement.

- Avoid cheesy clichés (e.g. 'for as long as I can remember') and over-use of quotations. One short quotation is acceptable if it is relevant and you comment on it.

- Do not include unsupported statements (e.g. 'I am hard-working'), which lack credibility. Instead, give evidence to support statements (e.g. things you have done which proved your capacity for hard work).
- Do not refer to specific courses as the same statement will go to all five of your university choices. You will not be able to write a convincing statement if you are applying to a variety of different courses (see below).
- Do not lie or exaggerate. You must be prepared to be questioned on anything you mention in your statement if you are called for interview.
- Do not try to be funny. Humour is very personal and can easily be misinterpreted or backfire.
- Do not be tempted to get someone else (a friend, teacher, parent or one of the many internet sites that offer 'help') to write your personal statement. It has to sound like you, which is why it is called a personal statement.

> **Caution!**
>
> Never, ever, copy and paste any part of your statement from any other sources (whether from a friend or the examples in this book or somewhere online). UCAS runs all applications through anti-plagiarism software. If you do this, you will be caught out and your application will be void.

Make sure you print out a copy of your personal statement when you have finished it so that you can refer to it again and remind yourself of the points that you raised, should you be called for interview.

As emphasised in Chapter 1, it is not necessary to study law at university in order to become a lawyer (although it saves you a year of study). This chapter focuses on applying to university to study law, but if you are applying for a non-law degree, exactly the same issues arise. Your personal statement should focus on why you wish to study your particular subject at university and why you are a good candidate.

> **Warning: mixing courses and joint honours courses**
>
> You will write only one personal statement, which is read by admissions staff at the five courses for which you are applying, so you must make sure that it is suitable for all five courses. Each university sees only its name and course code on the form that UCAS sends to it: your other choices are not revealed. So, if you are applying to read psychology at one university (remember, you do not have to read law at university to become a lawyer), management at another, history at a third, and so on, then you cannot possibly write

a personal statement that will satisfy the criteria for all of the courses. The psychology admissions tutor will wonder why you have written about history, and so on. The likelihood is that you will be rejected by all of your choices.

If you apply for a joint honours course such as law and French, your form will be seen by admissions tutors from both departments, each of whom will want to see that you are a serious candidate for his/her course. You must therefore cover both subjects in your statement.

ChatGPT and AI

The use of artificial intelligence (AI) software for crafting personal statements presents both advantages and drawbacks that require careful consideration.

While AI is adept at recognising patterns and generating text, it may lack the ability to produce creative and distinctive content, which is often essential for a standout personal statement. Plagiarism is also a concern; AI, in its automated processes, might inadvertently replicate existing personal statements or essays, raising questions about originality. And misrepresentation is a risk as well; AI, unintentionally, may introduce exaggerations or misrepresentations of an applicant's experiences or achievements, leading to ethical concerns and accuracy issues.

AI's limited contextual understanding is another challenge. It may struggle to grasp the specific requirements and nuances of a personal statement, potentially hindering the tailoring of the statement to the applied-for programme or institution. An over-reliance on AI could lead to a decline in critical thinking and writing skills, which are valuable beyond the application process in academic and professional contexts.

Thorough human editing is often necessary with AI-generated content to ensure accuracy, coherence and relevance. Neglecting this step can result in a subpar personal statement.

Finally, privacy concerns can arise, as some AI tools may store and use the data and content you input.

To mitigate these concerns, it is advisable to use AI software as a supplementary tool rather than the primary source of content. Give it clear and comprehensive commands to get the best results.

At the end of the day, the clue is 'personal' in the personal statement. Combining your own unique experiences and narrative with AI assistance to enhance grammar and clarity is important. Carefully review the AI-generated content to ensure that it genuinely reflects your attributes and aligns with the specific requirements of your application.

Tips from admissions tutors

The following advice has all been given by law admissions tutors at leading university law schools over the last few years.

Admissions tutors want to see that you have a genuine reason for wanting to study law and have made your decision to apply for a law degree based on thorough research. You must show that you have thought carefully about why you want to study for a law degree and have properly researched the degree programmes you are applying for. Do not list your achievements without explaining their applicability to a law degree. You should also have an idea of the different areas of law you can work in, although it is perfectly acceptable not to have made up your mind yet about which area you would prefer.

You also need to show that you have a firm grasp of current affairs and regularly read a quality newspaper. An up-to-date understanding of the legal profession is also important. Some admissions tutors consider an awarenessof current issues to be more important than reading law texts.

You should include any relevant work experience in your statement, although admissions tutors are very sensitive to the fact that not all students will have had the opportunity to get high-quality legal work experience. The general agenda to widen access to universities means that admissions tutors will make sure they avoid discriminating against applicants because of their background and the opportunities available to them. However, you still need to show what you have managed to do in the way of work experience and what you have learnt from it, even if it is not directly law related.

One important consideration for admissions tutors is the breadth of the application. In recent years, admissions tutors have commented on the fact that many applicants lack culture. While they may be committed to their studies or have undertaken a wealth of work experience, they don't often show their readiness to expand their knowledge, for example, by learning a new skill such as a language.

You should also:

- focus your personal statement on the course you are applying for
- make your personal statement sound like you
- apply early
- check carefully for spelling and grammatical errors.

Some sample personal statements for law degrees are shown below. Use these to get some ideas but **do not copy** any part of them into your own personal statement.

First sample personal statement *(3,938 characters)*

My desire to study law was initiated by my A level tutor whose passion was infectious. Since she had practised law as a barrister, she brought her experience within the courts to the theory of the A level curriculum. I became fascinated by tort law, in particular negligence. I was intrigued by the incremental developments in law and how it is often based on concerns surrounding public policy. The constant progression of the legal field attracts me.

I have taken the opportunity this year to study religious studies in an intensive one-year A level programme. This subject complements law due to the analytical and critical thinking skills it develops. I am particularly enjoying *Philosophy of Religion*, such as the cosmological argument, and look forward to studying natural moral law and ethics.

Retaking English Literature with a new board and entirely different texts is also preparing me well for undergraduate law; in the dystopian unit, Orwell's *1984* and Atwood's *The Handmaid's Tale* have encouraged me to question whether a state should remove the rights of an individual for the benefit of the regime, particularly one imposed; while *Hamlet* explores whether revenge for murder can ever be justified. Discussing characters facing ethical and legal dilemmas has provided different insights into the relationship between our personal and public lives that I hope to explore further at university.

Within my A level study of law, I was encouraged to consider different perspectives on claimant and defendants' rights and the potential injustices that may arise. For example, in the case of Collins v. Wilcock it was declared that a battery would be any intentional touching of another outside of the scope of what would be regarded as being normally acceptable. This was reinforced in the obiter comment in the case of R v. Chief Constable of Devon and Cornwall of 'even an unwanted kiss can be a battery'. These cases proved to me how developments in the law have the potential for a retrograde effect, as although the rights of the claimant were protected, it could lead to injustice for the defendant and the possibility of opening the floodgates with many new claims. The opportunity to debate broader implications of any act or judgement and the extent to which the legal system can bring about social justice appeals to me.

To gain insight into the legal profession, I have embarked on a year-long internship with a family law barrister, where I learn more about court proceedings. As further work experience I shadowed a KC judge in Derby Crown Court, where I gained experience by engaging with legal teams and judges and found myself within the dramatic proceedings of a criminal law trial. This taught me the necessity for precision and accuracy within the legal system.

Further work experience was gained in Nottingham and Coventry Magistrates' court, where I had the opportunity to achieve a mini pupillage. I was able to observe the court's procedures and the vast amount of organisation and strict preparation that is carried out every day throughout the works of a barrister.

Through LAMDA speech and drama qualifications, I developed confidence in public speaking and a high level of emotional intelligence, both key to professional success in the legal field. I showed commitment to a dance team for 10 years, participating in national competitions and utilising skills in tactical thinking and teamwork. Work experience at the BBC London enabled me to learn how the media handled stories with wider legal implications. I wrote a double-page article for my local newspaper regarding a charity cycling event that I organised, which was supported by over 200 cyclists and raised £30,000 for pancreatic cancer research.

I am genuinely excited at the prospect of starting university and studying a subject that I not only find enthralling but will enhance all the opportunities and experiences that university life may offer.

Second sample personal statement *(3,982 characters)*

Primarily my interest in studying undergraduate law began with my natural inquisitiveness into how the world works, particularly how laws are created and used to govern a society effectively. I have been exposed to legal affairs by sorting out my own tenancy agreement and ensuring that the contract's terms and agreements were correct. The implications of Brexit on society and our laws fascinates me greatly, especially as I am studying A level Politics. I am determined to increase my awareness of what's occurring in the world presently and historically as I believe this knowledge will benefit myself and the people I work with in the future.

I have a passionate interest in legal systems around the world, seeking to understand their effect on society. Taking A level Politics has allowed me to gain further insight into how laws are established in the US and the UK, but has also spurred further research into current political and legal affairs.

Discovering that the justification for the imprisonment of Nazanin Zaghari-Ratcliffe in Iran was spreading propaganda shocked me. From my research, I recognised the ambiguity of her accusation and wondered why her trial wasn't as clear cut as it should have been. Furthermore, it is a breach of her right to free speech and under the Iranian constitution free speech is a fundamental law. It made me wonder to what extent laws are influenced by religious and cultural beliefs, since laws are made for humans to abide by and yet in some regimes they are disregarded. This gave me insight into Catch 22s in which the laws in Iran must also abide by the principles of Islam, creating a paradoxical situation. Even in the text that I am studying in A level English Literature, *The Handmaid's Tale*, the ability of the theocratic government to override laws in the name of religion, despite violating fundamental human rights speaks volumes to me as I can see it happening in the world today.

Politics has also introduced me to the different powers of the judicial system in the US. The use of judicial review particularly interests me as it allows for reinterpretation of the Constitution. I realise that this can be considered as a positive aspect as the amendment process is especially difficult, but I also wonder if the Supreme Court is truly as unbiased as it is meant to be.

Even taking biology has enhanced my interest in legal cases due to discussion of ethical and legal implications of genetic modification, for example the Nuffield Council of Bioethics has green-lit that changing the DNA in a human embryo is 'morally permissible'. Biology has also improved my analytical skills and taught me the importance of precision in experiments.

A level English Literature has taken these evaluative skills even further, especially through studying *Hamlet* as I began to question the morality of revenge and the right to take law into our own hands. When given vast amounts of critical interpretations about the play, I have learned how to pick out necessary information efficiently and effectively for my upcoming exam and this will help me in the future when examining cases. In particular, the study of *1984* by George Orwell provided me with insight into different ideologies on how governments 'should' be run and how certain methods are detrimental to society. Although the focus was very much political, I contemplated how a legal system would come into play but there was obviously no such system in place. In this way, I recognised the importance of the legal system in protecting democracy.

Beyond the classroom, I have performed Bollywood dancing for charities that seek to educate about the importance of diversity. I learned how to communicate with people from diverse backgrounds and cultures. I believe the point of the legal system is to provide justice for individuals fairly and justly and look forward to exploring the precedents for this as part of a degree in law.

Third sample personal statement *(3,997 characters)*

Witnessing the establishment of a new constitution and parliament following the 2011 Egyptian Revolution, heightened my awareness of the rule of law. By 2015, Egypt had been functioning without a parliament for three years, causing stagnation and unrest. In contrast, the UK had a stable constitution founded on parliamentary sovereignty; ironically A.V. Dicey asserts there is 'no legal restraint' on Parliament's capacity, indicating that in theory even a sovereign legislature can spur instability. The distinction between Egypt and the UK intrigued me, heralding inevitable questions: who is responsible for creating our laws and applying them fairly in a state of flux? If the legislature cannot retain sovereignty due to extraneous factors, can the executive be trusted instead?

Hailing from Egypt, a civil law jurisdiction, I am fascinated by the UK's common law stimulating legislative progress. In my readings of R v R (1992), the House of Lords upheld a conviction of marital rape, setting a 'binding precedent'. I was thrilled to learn that public perceptions of morality could feed into justice, influencing judges to interpret the law in light of evolving social norms.

Interning in both civil and criminal law firms educated me on the practical application of the law. At Baker and McKenzie, I shadowed M&A solicitors as they clarified contractual terminology to clients and assisted in producing due diligence reports. At the criminal law practice, I observed barristers confute charges of insider trading and stock market manipulation, contextualising the overlap of criminal and corporate law.

I was further drawn to Law upon studying the US Civil Rights Movement; the NAACP recognised long-term social change could be prompted by legal reforms. Although, the often limited success of such measures introduced me to the dichotomy of dejure and defacto; the effectiveness of the verdicts of Plessy v Ferguson and Brown v Topeka was deliberated in our weekly Harkness debates, fortifying my ability to engage in Socratic discussions.

For my extended essay, I analysed justice and the law in Miller's 'The Crucible' and Shakespeare's 'The Merchant of Venice'. The former portrayed judges bound to religion, and the latter an executive influencing legal decisions. Both consolidated the need for an independent judiciary and impartiality through diversity, reinforcing my appreciation of Baroness Hale's appointment as well as the tie-break clause in the Constitutional Reform Act (2005). Similarly, my Maths IA explored gender parity in Parliament. Drawing parallels between literature, politics, history, maths and law will help me devise interdisciplinary legal arguments.

Getting into Law

> Attending King's College London's Law programme, I engaged in a mock trial arguing that a conviction based on the law of joint enterprise in R v Gnango should be upheld due to reasonable foreseeability, although this reasoning was later discredited in R v Jogee. Experience in mooting will assist me in forming and articulating legal interpretations for specific cases. As Head Girl, I evolved further as a public speaker. Moreover, writing a filmed screenplay on mental health enhanced my appreciation of the interplay of communicative mediums.
>
> Participating in the Model UN domestically and internationally refined my rhetoric and my cognizance of human rights. As delegate and International Court of Justice advocate, I employed the UDHR and ECHR as cornerstones for my arguments, specifically in the case of India v. Pakistan, contesting the Pakistani government's denial of consular access to Jadhav.
>
> My involvement in the renovation of an orphanage and a refugee educational programme, exposed the vulnerability of the marginalised under the selective justice of Egyptian law. Further research led me to KC Baroness Kennedy's campaign for substantive legal equality; 'Eve Was Framed' revealed that rape as a crime shouldn't be held to the threshold of beyond reasonable doubt. Kennedy inspires my academic curiosity and unwavering dedication to read Law.

The reference

For 2024 entry and beyond, a new system for references has been introduced in three distinct sections. The first is a general statement about the school or college. The second is to enter information about extenuating circumstances that may have impacted the student's academic performance. The third is for any information specific to the applicant that is relevant to the course that the university needs to be aware of. These should include:

- the student's suitability for the course and level of study
- an assessment of the student's academic performance to date
- how the student will adapt to university life
- the student's personal qualities.

If you are unsure as to whether the person who will write your reference fully understands what is required, show them the section on the UCAS website called 'Changes to undergraduate references for 2024 entry': www.ucas.com/advisers/help-and-training/guides-resources-and-training/writing-references/changes-undergraduate-references-2024-entry.

The LNAT

The LNAT is the National Admissions Test for Law. It is an externally set test which is used by a number of universities to help them select suitable candidates either for interview or for conditional offers. It does not test legal knowledge, but instead tests your aptitude for the skills required to study law, in particular:

- verbal reasoning
- ability to understand and interpret information
- ability to analyse information and draw conclusions
- deductive and inductive reasoning abilities.

The test lasts two-and-a-quarter hours and is in two sections – a multiple-choice section and an essay.

The multiple-choice section (95 minutes) is computer based and consists of 42 questions, based on passages of text setting out fictional scenarios. The score for this section is known as your LNAT score.

The essay section (40 minutes) tests your ability to construct logical, structured and clear arguments by writing one essay chosen from a list of essay questions. The essay is not actually marked by LNAT but is passed on to the participating universities with your LNAT score.

The best way to prepare yourself for the LNAT is to do several practice tests. The LNAT website (www.lnat.ac.uk) contains further details and also plenty of specimen questions and practice papers. There is also a practice test simulator that you can download. This is an on-screen simulation of the LNAT and includes a tutorial and two live practice tests. These will allow you to familiarise yourself with the format of the test and the skills it requires.

The multiple-choice section is based on fairly substantial passages of text, and examples of this section can be found on the LNAT website. However, below are some examples of the sort of essay questions you might be asked, with more examples available on the LNAT website.

1. In what circumstances should abortion be permitted and why?
2. Would you agree that travel and tourism exploit poorer nations and benefit only the richer ones?
3. Wearing a burkha in Western countries is just as offensive as wearing a bikini in Arab countries. Do you agree?

The LNAT is used by the following UK universities at the time of writing:

- University of Bristol
- University of Cambridge
- Durham University
- University of Glasgow

- King's College London
- London School of Economics and Political Science (LSE)
- University of Nottingham
- University of Oxford
- SOAS, University of London
- University College London (UCL).

In 2023, registration for the LNAT opened on 1 August, with testing beginning on 1 September. However, the deadlines for registering and booking the LNAT and for sitting the test differed from institution to institution. Meeting these deadlines is crucial to ensure that your LNAT application is considered, so it is essential you check the specific details with your chosen universities.

Other key points associated with the LNAT:

- The test is sat at an external test centre.
- The current cost of the test is £75 at UK and EU test centres, and £120 for other centres. The fee is payable online by credit or debit card at the time of booking.
- You can sit the test only once in any application cycle. If you sit it a second time, the later result will not count.
- If you reapply in subsequent years to universities that require the LNAT, you will have to sit the LNAT again.
- Candidates who may need extra time (for example, students with dyslexia) or need special arrangements (for example, students with sight or mobility problems) should register for the LNAT online, but should not book their test online. Documentary evidence must be supplied. Further information can be found on the LNAT website.

Case study

After securing three A* grades at A level, Julia accepted a place at the University of Southampton to study LLB Law. She has recently commenced her first year of the course, having deferred her place for a year.

'The academic rigour of studying law was very appealing to me. I find the scope of law fascinating and chose the University of Southampton for its reputation for academic research; it has unique ties with the Institute of Maritime Law and the Stefan Cross Centre for Women, Equality and Law, both of which we have the option to engage with over the duration of the course. Although it is early days for me, I intend to work in the law clinic that the university runs and utilise the marshalling schemes that will give me first-hand exposure to the work of barristers and judges. I am also keen to engage with outreach programmes to educate people on their rights in specific areas.

'As well as having a nice campus, the strength of the contacts at Southampton, as well as its relative proximity to my hometown, ultimately led me to choosing it. I had initially wanted to study at a London university, but decided that the high costs could be a hindrance.

'I want to try and use my summer breaks to get work experience and vacation schemes with big firms or chambers. In order to be considered, I had to study for the LNAT, which was very time consuming, but the wider reading and practice that I did helped to develop my critical thinking skills and my broader knowledge of how law impacts daily life. The LNAT website recommends some books to read and provides plenty of resources – and these worked for me. They also advise against going on LNAT courses and having any formal training, as it really isn't needed.

'Even before the pandemic, I had decided to take a gap year, and had planned to do voluntary work in Calais. I was fortunate enough to spend some time there before commencing my studies, but not being able to travel as planned actually worked out in my favour, as I was able to get a paid job in a law firm as a junior legal assistant in residential conveyancing. My tasks on a day-to-day basis involved maintaining filing systems and taking phonecalls, but I was able to liaise with many people working in the profession and gain a strong insight into what the role of a solicitor entails.

'At this point, I don't know what I want to do in terms of my career after my law degree. There are so many options and I don't yet feel I have seen enough to have made a decision. I intend to get a lot more experience and perhaps even undertake postgraduate study before committing.'

Fictional Harvard Law grad Frank Underwood was a President who resigned from office on what Netflix series?

Answer: House of Cards

8 | Burden of proof: Succeeding at interview

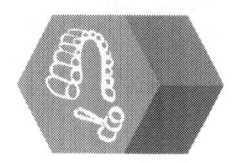

Outside Oxford and Cambridge, formal interviews are rarely part of the admissions process for law degrees. Most universities, even those in the highly respected Russell Group of top universities, do not interview candidates for law degrees at all, other than those with unusual qualifications or mature students. In these cases, the universities interview because they need more information to help them make a decision. One notable exception at the time of writing is the University of Bristol, which does interview applicants; as much of their programme delivery is through problem-based learning, Bristol uses the interview as an opportunity to assess the relevant skills that cannot be demonstrated on the UCAS form. Oxford and Cambridge also interview all applicants, though Oxford is still using online interviews. If you are invited to attend an academic interview, this chapter contains some guidance on what to expect at the interview and how you might be able to prepare.

You may also be invited to an interview for work experience at a firm of solicitors or set of barristers' chambers. Much of the advice in this chapter is equally relevant to this situation and the same recommendations also apply. A few additional tips that apply particularly to interviews for work experience are given near the end of the chapter.

> **Oxford and Cambridge examples**
>
> Guides to interviews, including sample questions and video examples, are available on the websites of Oxford and Cambridge universities.
>
> - www.ox.ac.uk/admissions/undergraduate/applying-to-oxford/guide/interviews
> - www.undergraduate.study.cam.ac.uk/applying/interviews

What to expect at the interview

The purpose of an interview is to test your:

- motivation to study law
- logical reasoning ability
- effective communication skills.

The university is not seeking to test your prior knowledge of the law.

You are likely to be asked questions on the following:

- why you wish to study law
- why you wish to go to that particular university
- your academic qualifications
- the personal statement in your UCAS form
- some questions on legal issues which are designed to assess your logical reasoning and communication skills.

You will also be asked whether there is anything you would like to ask your interviewer.

Interviews need not be daunting – they are just conversations with people who know a lot about your chosen subject. They are designed to help those asking the questions to find out as much about you as they can. Interviewers are more interested in what you know than in what you do not.

The interview is a chance for you to demonstrate your commitment to and enthusiasm for the law. Interviewers clearly wish to know your reasons for wanting to study law and, possibly above all, they will be looking to see whether you have a mind capable of developing logical arguments and the ability to articulate such arguments powerfully and coherently. You should view an interview as a chance to put yourself across well rather than as an obstacle course designed to catch you out.

Preparation for a law interview

Once you have been asked to attend an interview, it is sensible to prepare thoroughly. You should take the time to think through your answers to some of the questions you are likely to be asked. You should also be very well informed about the course you are applying for and any current legal issues which you might be asked about. Try to arrange some mock interviews, carried out by a teacher at school, careers advisor, family friend, or anyone else you can persuade to help. These can be very useful. Reeling off pre-prepared answers to questions is obviously not going to impress an interviewer, but thinking in advance about what you are likely to be asked about can help you get your thoughts in order and sound confident and prepared at the interview.

Re-read your personal statement

You are very likely to be asked questions about your personal statement, so read it through well before the interview and make sure you can remember and speak coherently about any books you mentioned having read. If you have followed the advice contained in Chapter 7 of this book, you will not have included anything in your statement that you are not prepared to speak about at interview. Take a copy of the statement with you to the interview and read it through again shortly beforehand.

Why do you want to study law?

This is an obvious question and you should think about your reasons carefully before the interview. Reasons for wishing to study law vary. A passion for television courtroom drama series is not enough. You need to think about the everyday practice of the law in this country and it is very useful to spend time talking with lawyers of all kinds and learning what is involved. You may well be asked whether you have spoken to any lawyers about their work or visited any courts.

In terms of answering the question at interview, it is crucial that you convey a genuine interest in studying law. Often, your response will be in line with your personal statement. There are several possible aspects that you could cover when answering this question.

- An interest in law that has stemmed from a genuine interest in political affairs and the legal system. You might have followed some cases closely that you found particularly interesting, or read a book that piqued your interest. You need to be prepared to provide specifics here, and to answer questions on the things that you mention as evidence to support your answers.
- An event that occurred may have motivated you to pursue a degree or a career in law. This could be witnessing a lawyer represent someone you know, or perhaps even observing a perversion of the course of justice that you want to help overcome. It is important that these narratives are true, as you will need to be able to convey your resulting enthusiasm convincingly and be able to answer any related questions that an interviewer might have.
- It may have been a work experience placement or a conversation with a lawyer that stimulated your interest. You should consider exactly what it was that got your attention – a specific element of the work a lawyer was conducting that you found interesting, or a role that you were allowed to support with that you enjoyed. Lawyers can carry out a wide range of tasks, so reflect carefully on all elements of the job and the kind of environment in which they work.
- You may want to study law for the academic challenge that it represents as opposed to the career prospects. If this is the real motivator, then you should consider the ways in which the course

- will stretch your capabilities and the skills that it will allow you to develop. Highlight any modules of particular interest, and explain why they interest you.
- The skills that you have may lend themselves well to the study of law, and reflecting on them at this point could strengthen your case. It is important to be modest, though – resist the urge to exaggerate!

It is important to be aware of the many types of law that lawyers practise – criminal, contract, family, taxation, etc. – and be clear about the differences between them. You may be asked what areas of law you are particularly interested in or whether you hope to become a barrister or solicitor (although you would not be expected to have come to any firm decisions at this stage). You should be clear in your mind about the difference between them.

Never talk about how much you expect to earn, or demonstrate any passivity about your decision to study law. Your parents making the suggestion for you to do so, following a family tradition or watching TV shows, are also unlikely to make a good case for obtaining an offer.

Many interviewers will also expect you to answer a question along the lines of 'Why should we offer you a place?' These questions often arise towards the end of an interview, and therefore provide a useful opportunity for you to summarise the key points that you have covered in your interview, highlighting the reasons why you want to study law, your skills, what you have to offer and reasons for choosing that particular university. It is also worth discussing how you might be able to contribute to other aspects of university life, including extra-curricular activities such as sports and music. It might also be useful to discuss any ways in which you have contributed to your school community, such as organising charity events or participating in clubs and societies.

Make sure you know all about the course and the university

Read through all the information on the university's website relevant to the course you have chosen and also read any brochures or other written information you may have been given at any open day you attended.

A common question early on in an interview is why you chose to apply for that particular university. It is important to look carefully at the information available on the course. If there is a particular element of the course that differs from others, reflect on it. For example, a university may have a very well-established research department if you are interested in academia, while others may have a particular emphasis on work experience and provide good links to assist students in securing placements. Or there might be a specific module on offer, delivered by a specialist in the area, in which you have a particular interest.

The reputation of the department will typically be a determining factor in choosing a university, but it is also worth investigating the approach to teaching. Some of the more academic universities expect a greater degree of independent work, while others offer more support. Some universities deliver sessions using problem-based learning, which can be an excellent way of developing your skills, but it is not suitable for everyone.

Mentioning aspects such as the local excellent nightlife is not recommended, even if it did influence your decision initially! Law is an incredibly demanding course, and interviewers and admissions officers won't want to hear about potential distractions.

Practise getting the right body language

This is not as obvious as it seems, so a small amount of practice will make all the difference. Use mock interviews to give you some practice of walking into a room, looking your interviewer in the eyes, smiling, saying hello and shaking their hand. The handshake should be firm and confident – but without crushing their fingers. Sit down upright in your seat and do not slouch or lean back too far. You want to look interested and engaged and also relaxed, but not overly casual.

Be informed about current affairs

Reading a quality daily newspaper will keep you up to date with current legal issues and how they are reported in the media. Issues relating to politics, the police, sentencing and prison reform are possible interview topics.

Quality newspapers, such as the *Independent*, *The Times* and the *Guardian* all report on current legal issues and give you insight into important legal cases. You could also read *The Law Society Gazette* or *The Lawyer*, which are published weekly in print format and are also available online. *The Law Society Gazette* contains reviews of current legal issues and matters affecting the legal profession. *The Lawyer* tends to focus more on news and comment about comings and goings in the legal profession (such as mergers between law firms); it also has an online litigation tracker which holds over 9,000 cases with data points including counsel, law firms, judges, clients and sectors that are all fully searchable, which can be incredibly useful when researching current affairs.

Many current issues discussed on radio and television have legal implications. Watching or listening to *Question Time*, *Newsnight* and certain *Panorama*-style documentaries and Radio 4's *Today* programme, *The World This Weekend* and *Today in Parliament* will enable you to develop a thorough knowledge of current affairs. You could also visit the legal websites mentioned in the 'Further information' chapter at the end of the book.

In preparing for an interview, you should consider wider questions such as:

- What do you think should be happening in the prison system at the moment?
- What reforms would you like to see implemented in the running of the police force?

To be confident in presenting your opinions, it is helpful to discuss such issues with friends or family and then practise answering the questions at mock interviews.

In addition to discussing specific cases and legal reforms, it is highly likely that recent political events will form part of the interview. Politics can change rapidly – no one predicted a General Election in 2017, for example – so it is vital that you stay well informed.

Outlined below are themes prominent in the political and legal sphere at the time of writing. Remember, this is just a rough guide as opposed to an exhaustive list – it is up to you to stay abreast of current affairs.

Brexit

The legal implications of the UK's departure from the EU on 31 January 2020 should be closely followed by any prospective lawyer. You may be asked to discuss the impact of Brexit on parliamentary sovereignty and also on the UK's legal system. Aspects to consider include:

- the impact of the UK's decision to leave the EU on parliamentary sovereignty and the power of the judiciary
- the Miller cases (2017 and 2019) and the implications these have for parliamentary sovereignty, governmental authority and the legal landscape.

Not only has Brexit resulted in unprecedented levels of political uncertainty, it has seen legal channels being used to hold the government to account in a way that has arguably shifted public perception of the UK's Supreme Court. Three key cases are explored below.

Cases to consider

R (Miller) v. the Secretary of State for Exiting the European Union (2017) is a legal case where the UK government was taken to court over its handling of Brexit. The premise of the case was that the Cabinet were neglecting the principle of parliamentary sovereignty as they made the decision to trigger Article 50 without a parliamentary vote. As a result of the court case, the UK's Supreme Court ruled there must be a vote within both chambers prior to triggering Article 50.

> **Cherry and others (Respondents) v. Advocate General for Scotland (Appellant) (Scotland)** and **R (on the application of Miller) (Appellant) v. The Prime Minister (Respondent)** are both cases that attracted a great deal of attention regarding Brexit negotiations. Following Boris Johnson's decision to prorogue (suspend) Parliament, two cases were brought to the Supreme Court, first in Scotland and then in England.
>
> This was due to questions surrounding the legality of Johnson's decision to prorogue Parliament – while prorogation is a routine event, the issue with this request was that it was for an extended period of time, which limited the time available to MPs to debate and give their input on EU withdrawal arrangements, as well as preventing decisions being made regarding the way in which the UK would exit the EU. Many saw the decision to prorogue Parliament and prevent MPs from sitting in a crucial period in the run up to the Brexit deadline as a way for Johnson to exit without a deal. In addition, many felt that the Prime Minister had misadvised the Queen, but it is important to note that the monarch does not have a discretion, and the system is premised on the Prime Minister honestly advising the Queen in the country's best interest. As such, there was a huge amount of political opposition surrounding the decision from both opposing parties and MPs within the Conservative Party. In Cherry v. Advocate General for Scotland, the court found that the Prime Minister had not been acting unlawfully in suspending Parliament. Conversely, in R v. The Prime Minister, it was found that prorogation was unlawful and that Parliament should reconvene immediately. This shows that any given situation can be open to an element of interpretation by judges, especially when they are acting in such an unprecedented context.

When reflecting on the above cases, it is important to consider the implications of utilising legal frameworks to hold a government to account. You should consider the arguments for and against the decision of the plaintiff to launch the case.

It is also worth considering the media coverage of these cases. After the 2017 Miller case the tabloid *Daily Mail* dubbed the Supreme Court judges that came to the decision 'the enemies of the people', raising some interesting perceptions about the legal profession. Some might potentially view such judges as acting 'ultra vires', or beyond one's power. You should consider whether unelected individuals should have the power to hold a government to account or not.

Although the Brexit date is now well in the past, it is important to keep a close eye on the news to follow updates as they occur. With over 1,000 laws already revoked and 600 possible revisions, there is still much to consider.

Environmentalism

The Paris Accord (2014) established legal expectations regarding emissions reductions which all signatories must abide by. With the UK's fourth carbon budget fast approaching, environmentalism and the necessity of a low-carbon future are prominent themes at present. Concerns about the environment and air quality have intersected with the legal sphere, as seen by the multiple cases brought forward against the government by organisations such as ClientEarth. Some possible aspects to consider include the following.

- The culpability of governments with regard to air quality. You should consider whether or not you believe the government can be held liable.
- Issues associated with green crime and environmental laws and the challenges involved in deciding culpability and accountability.
- Whether the ClientEarth cases set a new legal precedent and what can be done in cases where there is no direct or clear victim.
- Cases brought against those who have protested using direct action, such as the Heathrow 13 or anti-fracking protesters.

Climate change

Climate change represents an unprecedented global crisis, demanding a robust and comprehensive legal response. Climate-focused litigation is poised to expand its influence across both the public and private sectors of the legal landscape. As a result, companies will increasingly find themselves held accountable for ecological harm, environmental transgressions, and corporate responsibility for mitigating climate-related risks. Legal actions in this arena will span various aspects, including liability for greenhouse gas emissions, damage to natural resources, and corporate obligations to address climate change.

To complicate matters further, law firms must undergo a transformation in their practices and operations to align with the urgent need to address climate change. This transformation goes beyond mere token gestures; it requires a genuine commitment to eco-consciousness. As a part of this commitment, law firms can adopt measures such as transitioning to paperless office environments, establishing office supply recycling programmes, and embedding sustainable practices into their day-to-day operations. Additionally, providing pro bono legal support to environmental organisations and communities affected by climate change represents a meaningful way for law firms to contribute to positive change and address this pressing issue. By actively embracing these practices, law firms can take a leadership role in creating a more environmentally sustainable and resilient future while navigating the evolving legal landscape shaped by climate-related issues.

The judicial branch in the USA

When appointed as 45th President of the United States, one of the first things that Donald Trump was able to do was appoint a member to the Supreme Court. This is a power that all US Presidents have held, yet their ability to use it depends entirely on a vacancy occurring as a result of either death, retirement or gross misconduct resulting in impeachment as Supreme Court justices are granted tenure for life. The life tenure raises concerns that the court could potentially serve as an echo chamber for presidential views, which could be indicative of the President having too much power.

Given that this differs significantly from the UK judicial system, it is certainly worth researching.

White-collar crime

Another area of interest is crime committed by the wealthy. These crimes are often corporate in nature and the term 'white-collar crime' can be applied.

As with green crimes, white-collar crimes are often difficult to prove as they tend to have no direct victim, and often there is very little delineation between legal and illegal behaviours. Take for instance the concepts of tax avoidance and tax evasion – one of them is completely legal, while the other is not.

There is a great degree of interest about how the wealthy and elite within society move their money, often as a means to avoid taxation. The widespread nature of such practices came to light in the Panama Papers in 2015 and, more recently, in the Paradise Papers in 2017. It is well worth considering the legal implications of both these papers.

While exploring the low conviction rates for white-collar crime, it is worth considering the concerns that exist regarding the disproportionate number of working-class people within the prison population, and the ability of the middle classes to get away with criminal activity. Exploring this area could be augmented through researching the works of the theorists Snider and Chambliss.

Aspects to consider include:

- the administration of fair justice
- the issue of diversity in the legal profession. Since law is the profession with the highest proportion of privately educated individuals, you could consider whether this may cause barriers to other individuals accessing the legal profession, as well as whether this lack of diversity has an impact on conviction rates.

Terrorism and anti-terror legislation

Concerns about the compatibility of the Human Rights Act with anti-terrorism legislation focus on how a major terrorist threat can be used to restrict people's civil rights and liberties. Consider whether you believe that human rights should be suspended or limited in the face of a terrorist threat and how this interacts with the notion of judicial precedents. If contexts are constantly changing, is it better for the judiciary to consider things on a case-by-case basis?

AI

Earlier this year, Allen & Overy announced a partnership with the artificial intelligence platform ChatGPT in order to help its lawyers complete their legal tasks. Artificial intelligence, which mimics specific operations of the human mind, is the term used to describe computer programmes capable of completing tasks that typically require human intelligence. AI definitely has a place in the legal profession – but what exactly?

Law firms are acutely conscious of the impact of emerging legal technology. Many of these firms aspire to be pioneers in integrating it into their future growth strategies. Nonetheless, they are equally committed to ensuring that technology, particularly AI, does not supplant human involvement in addressing legal issues.

AI has the potential to be employed for tasks like document review, legal research, assisting in due diligence, contract examination and management, forecasting legal outcomes, and streamlining recruitment procedures.

According to Deloitte's projections, automation is expected to eliminate around 100,000 legal positions by 2036. Hence, the imperative for all law firms is to embrace AI readiness at this juncture.

Jodie and Mary

In the year 2000, the story of conjoined twins, Jodie and Mary, made headline news. The key question was whether it was ethically acceptable to separate them, even if it meant that the weaker twin, Mary, might not survive. Both twins were destined for a premature death if they remained joined. While the parents wanted to keep them together, doctors needed legal permission for the separation. In a complex mix of ethical and legal challenges, Lord Justice Ward stated, 'this is a court of law, not a court of ethics'.

After much deliberation and sleepless nights, the judges eventually allowed the separation. Lord Justice Brooke justified it as a matter of necessity, choosing the option with the least harm. The stronger twin, Jodie, not only survived but also fully recovered. This unique case, often discussed in philosophy, highlights the intricate relationship between legal principles and moral dilemmas, a central topic in legal theory courses.

Current affairs

Current affairs are constantly changing, which is why it is so important to stay up to date. Other aspects that are in the media at present include:

- cases pertaining to historic sex abuse (including rape victims having to hand over their mobile phones or risk having their cases dropped)
- prison riots and deaths in custody
- the effectiveness of different methods of administering justice: rehabilitative, retributive, punitive and restorative
- LGBTQ+ rights, parental rights and gender
- No-fault divorce (Owens v. Owens case).

It is recommended that you add to this list as and when new topics present themselves in the news.

In addition to keeping a close eye on current affairs, compile a list of five to ten cases that you can discuss in both your personal statement and at interview. It would be a good idea to group these in themes. For example, the transformative power of the law regarding civil rights would be likely to include cases such as Brown v. Board of Education (1954); whereas cases regarding the rights of African Americans with Affirmative Action cases might include the recent case of Fisher v. University of Texas. Whichever cases you choose, ensure you know the facts and are able to express an informed opinion.

Joint degree subjects

If you have chosen a joint or combined honours course, then obviously you will have to prepare yourself for questions on the other subject you are hoping to study alongside law as well as questions on law.

Questions on legal issues

Knowledge of the structure of the legal and judicial systems is vital. Read Chapter 2 of this book to give you a basic understanding of the legal system. You should know who the Lord Chief Justice is, who the Director of Public Prosecutions is and what he or she does. You should be aware of recent controversial legal decisions, who took them and what their consequences are or could be. Who is the Home Secretary and why is he or she important?

Interviewers will ask questions with a view to being in a position to form an opinion about the quality of your thought and your ability to argue a particular case. You may be presented with a real or supposed set of circumstances and then be asked to comment on the legal implications of them. Is euthanasia wrong? What is the purpose of prison?

At the end of this chapter there are some sample questions, which show the type of legal questions you may be asked. Questions may be straightforward and specific, but can also involve more convoluted scenarios for you to think through. Remember that there are no right or wrong answers – you simply need to show that you can think through the issues in a logical and reasoned way and communicate your arguments and conclusions effectively.

Online versus in-person interviews

In reality, there is little difference between an online and an in-person interview beyond the delivery of it. Therefore, the majority of advice in this chapter is pertinent to candidates attending both types. Where people struggle with online interviews is that they can be disorientating – often interviewees become too relaxed, as they are taking them in familiar surroundings. You can avoid that by choosing to carry out the online interview in more formal – not to mention quiet – surroundings, such as an empty classroom. Treat your laptop screen as if it actually is the interviewer, not simply a projection. Shut off other means of communication and, if possible, ensure there is a blank wall behind the screen so you have no other distractions. Do not have your notes or books around you in the hope they will give you an advantage – it will be obvious and you will be flustered.

On the day: practicalities and general advice

Arrive (or log on) early

Make sure you know where you are going and leave plenty of time to get there. Allow for trains and buses to be delayed. Make sure your phone is fully charged before you leave home and that you have located your destination on a map. Also make sure you take the telephone number of the admissions office so that if, despite your best efforts, you are late, you can phone and let them know. Remember to re-read your personal statement just before the interview.

Dress carefully

Dress comfortably, but show that you are taking the interview seriously: wear smart, clean clothes. You should also clean your shoes and make sure your hair is neat. The same applies if you are taking an online interview – it is all about being in the right mindset.

Be calm

Take a few deep breaths before the interview and, if you are nervous, try to calm and relax yourself. Listen to a favourite piece of music or

Getting into Law

something that you know will make you feel more relaxed. Remember you wouldn't have been invited for interview unless you were a serious candidate for a place, so be confident and let your talents shine through!

Demeanour during the interview

- Be yourself.
- Be enthusiastic and show a strong commitment to your subject.
- Maintain good eye contact with your interviewer(s) and confident body language.
- Listen carefully to the questions you are asked and make sure you understand what you are being asked before you answer. Don't be afraid to ask questions if you are unsure of what the interviewer wants.
- In online interviews, switch off the camera view of yourself, and look at the interviewer only.
- Be concise and logical – put forward your answer and use examples and factual knowledge to reinforce your points.
- If you are asked a question you don't know the answer to, say so. To waffle simply wastes time and lets you down. To lie, of course, is even worse – especially for aspiring lawyers!
- Be willing to consider new ideas, if your interview involves discussion of legal or other current issues. An ability to see the opposite point of view while maintaining your own will mark you out as strong law degree material.
- Show a willingness to learn and be prepared to admit defeat if you put forward an argument that is demolished by your interviewer. A touch of humility will not hurt.

An ability to think on your feet is vital – another prerequisite for a good lawyer. Although you will (hopefully) have thought through answers to some of the questions you are likely to be asked, you do not want to sound as though you are reeling off a pre-learned answer as this will sound false and will not impress anyone.

Much of the practice of law in this country rests on an adversarial system, so don't be surprised if you receive an adversarial interview.

Remember to keep calm and think clearly!

Think of some questions to ask your interviewer(s)

At the end of the interview, you will almost certainly be given the chance to ask if you have any questions. It is sensible to have one or two questions of a serious kind – to do with the course, the tuition and so on – up your sleeve. It is not wise, obviously, to ask them anything that you could and should have found out from the prospectus. If there is nothing, then say that your interview has covered all that you had thought of.

Above all, end on a positive note and remember to smile!

The interview for work experience

Most of the advice in this chapter will equally apply if you are going for an interview for work experience to a firm of solicitors or a set of chambers. However, in addition you should do the following.

- Research the firm/chambers thoroughly before interview. Look at their brochure and website.
- Plan in advance what you think your key selling points are to the employer and make sure you find an opportunity in the interview to get your points across.
- Prepare a few questions about the firm to ask your interviewer at the end. You can demonstrate your preparation here by asking them about something you have read about the firm/chambers recently, if appropriate.
- Dress smartly and appropriately. Lawyers tend to look quite formal, so a suit is probably appropriate in this situation.

Sample interview questions on legal issues

Here are a few sample legal questions which show the type of thing you may be asked.

1. Should cannabis be legalised?
2. Is there legal precedent to go to war?
3. Do lawyers have an ethical responsibility to leverage AI (artificial intelligence) in the practice of law?
4. What are the pros and cons of fusing the two branches of the legal profession?
5. Is ChatGPT a useful tool in legal research?
6. Should the police in this country be armed?
7. If you were in a position of power, would you change the current civil legal aid situation?
8. Should the police spend their time enforcing the laws concerned with begging?
9. Tell me what you understand about the Paris Agreement and the US withdrawal.
10. What do you think of recent law reforms?
11. Are strikes in public sector jobs lawful?
12. What are your views on the right to silence?
13. How can you quantify compensation for victims of crime?
14. Should criminals be allowed to sell their stories as 'exclusives'?
15. How does the law affect your daily life?
16. What would happen if there were no law?
17. Is it necessary for the law to be entrenched in archaic tradition, ritual and jargon?

18. How are law and morality related?
19. Do you believe that all people have equal access to justice?
20. What is justice?
21. Why do we send criminals to prison? What are the alternatives?
22. Should the media be more careful with the way in which they report crime?
23. Do you think the press should be allowed to report the names of celebrities when unproven allegations of sexual abuse have been made against them?
24. Is law the best way to handle situations such as domestic violence/child abuse/rape?
25. What causes crime rates to increase?
26. Is trial by jury a good idea? Should anyone be allowed to serve on a jury?
27. Do you think capital punishment should be reinstated?
28. Should the law permit suspected terrorists to be held indefinitely without trial?
29. If shoplifting were punishable by death, and therefore nobody did it, would that be a just and effective law?
30. You are driving along a busy road with the window down when a swarm of bees flies into your car. You panic and lose control of the car, causing a huge pile-up. Are you legally responsible?
31. A blind person, travelling by train, gets out at his/her destination. Unfortunately the platform is shorter than the train, and the blind person falls to the ground, sustaining several injuries. Who, if anyone, should compensate him/her?
32. A cyclist rides the wrong way down a one-way street and a chimney falls on him. What legal proceedings should he take? What if he is riding down a private drive signed 'no trespassing'?

What is the age of criminal responsibility in England and Wales?

Answer: 10 years old

9 | Letter of the law: Non-standard applications

Not all of those who become lawyers decide on that career at an early age. Many successful lawyers are people who started out on a completely different career path. Equally, a number of successful lawyers in the UK come from overseas. Law firms and chambers welcome applicants from a wide range of backgrounds, and often have diversity initiatives in place. This chapter offers a brief overview of non-standard applications. For more information, please check with individual universities or the professional representative bodies for solicitors and barristers – i.e. the Law Societies of England and Wales, Scotland and Northern Ireland or, for aspiring barristers, the Bar Council of England and Wales, the Faculty of Advocates in Scotland or the Bar of Northern Ireland. Website addresses for all these institutions are given in Chapter 12.

Graduates with degrees other than law

Many lawyers, particularly in England and Wales, have obtained a degree in a subject other than law. As is explained more fully in the relevant sections of Chapter 4, this simply necessitates taking a further postgraduate qualification in law in order to cover the material that would usually be studied during a law degree. This qualification is the GDL in England and Wales, a two-year accelerated law degree in Scotland and a Master's in Law in Northern Ireland. The additional qualification is taken before moving on to the vocational stage of training. Please see the relevant sections of Chapter 4 for more information. Many employers positively welcome applications from non-law graduates, with the different range of skills that they bring. There are, however, financial implications as the additional years of study will need to be funded.

Mature students

Many law firms and sets of chambers positively welcome new recruits who are embarking on law as a second career. Experience or knowledge of particular business or industry sectors which form a law firm's client base can be especially welcomed. For example, former medical practitioners have the knowledge and experience to become excellent medical negligence lawyers. Many lawyers have not gone straight from school and university to the legal profession.

The possible routes for mature students to enter the legal profession depend on their level of academic qualifications.

Mature students who have a degree in a subject other than law are in the same position as other non-law graduates and are eligible to take the SQE, or its equivalent outside England and Wales.

Mature students who do not have a degree can, if they can satisfy the entry requirements (i.e. they have A level or equivalent qualifications), contact the SRA to determine whether they would be eligible to take the SQE. While there is no specific requirements to have a law degree, it would be a good idea to undertake some formal study in law in preparation for qualifying, as a thorough understanding will be required to pass the SQE.

Mature students without A levels (or equivalent qualifications) would need to take an Access to Higher Education course at a local further education college before applying to university. Each year around 20,000 Access to HE students apply for a degree course at a UK university to study subjects including law. In Scotland, a different system, called the Scottish Wider Access Programme, operates and Northern Irish universities have their own arrangements for access courses. More details are available at www.accesstohe.ac.uk.

Some universities offer law degrees with a Foundation year. These courses are designed to allow prospective lawyers without formal qualifications to gain access onto the course. The requirements for entry vary between universities, but applications tend to be considered from those who have completed the Access to Higher Education course, mature learners with no formal qualifications and young learners who have not undertaken post-16 qualifications. A list of providers and their entry requirements can be found on the UCAS website.

Alternatively, there are non-graduate routes to becoming a lawyer (see Chapter 4). For example, the solicitors' profession in England and Wales offers a unified route with the roll-out of the SQE. Non-graduate routes to qualifying are also available in Scotland (see page 70) and Northern Ireland (see page 73).

Overseas students

Overseas students who already have a degree in their own country may apply to either the Solicitors Regulation Authority (for aspiring solicitors) or the Bar Standards Board (for barristers) for a certificate of academic standing, which will then allow them to take the SQE in England and Wales, possibly following a period of postgraduate legal training or taking a standalone SQE preparation course, in the same way as non-law graduates (see above).

Solicitors who have trained in a different country and wish to practise in England or Wales will need to undertake the SQE, which replaces the Qualified Lawyers Transfer Scheme (QLTS).

Alternatively, overseas students might wish to start their training to become a UK lawyer by applying to study for their degree at a UK university. If you are in this situation, then the advice and guidance contained in Chapters 6 and 7 applies equally to you. However, the statistics show that overseas students are a lot less successful than UK students in gaining places at UK universities to read law, as the Law Society's figures for 2022 entry show:

Applicants' nationality	Number of applicants	Places	% Success
UK	31,585	21,650	68.5%
Overseas	9,330	4,640	49.7%

Table 6: Nationality and success rate for university law degree courses

This section therefore includes particular advice for overseas applicants on applying to a UK university to read law.

The process of applying as an international student is similar to that used by UK students: you use the same online UCAS form, provide the same information, and have the same deadlines. The differences are likely to be these:

- the examinations you have taken and/or will be taking may not appear in the drop-down menus on the UCAS form
- the fee codes and support arrangements will be different
- your school may not have registered with UCAS and so you may have to apply as a private individual rather than through an institution.

Detailed advice about how to fill in the UCAS form, and to deal with these issues, can be found in the 'Applying to University' section of the UCAS website (www.ucas.com). This section of the UCAS website contains special advice for international students for each section of the UCAS form. There is also a summary of tips for international students (www.ucas.com/undergraduate/applying-university/ucas-undergraduate-international-and-eu-students).

However, many well-qualified, serious and motivated international students are unsuccessful in their applications because they or their referees (or both) are unfamiliar with what the university selectors are looking for in two particular sections of the application form:

1. the personal statement
2. the reference.

The personal statement

Students who have applied for universities outside of the UK may be familiar with the idea of writing a statement about themselves to support their applications. These can often take the form of a 'hard sell', in which the student extols his or her personal qualities, achievements, hopes and dreams. This format is not suitable for a UCAS personal statement, which needs to focus on the course itself, and what the student has done to investigate it. The advice given in Chapter 7 is equally applicable to international students, and you should read it carefully. The UCAS website also recommends that you should specifically mention in your personal statement why you want to study in the UK, your English language skills (and any tests or courses you have taken) and why you do not want to study in your own country.

The reference

Referees for overseas students will need to follow the same systemn as for UK applicants (see page 113). However, the referee should also provide an assessmen of the student's level of English if this is not his or her first language and how the student will adapt to studying in the UK.

LNAT

Some universities require candidates to sit the Law National Admissions Test (LNAT) in addition to gaining academic qualifications. This online test can be sat outside of the UK. See Chapter 7, page 125 for more details.

Academic qualifications

The UCAS website (www.ucas.com) gives details of the acceptable non-UK qualifications. The international sections on individual university websites will provide further details. International students whose local qualifications are not acceptable to UK universities will need to study A levels or the equivalent either at an international school in their own country or at a school or college in the UK, or possibly follow a one-year university Foundation course. Details of providers of UK qualifications can be found on the British Council website (https://study-uk.british-council.org).

9 Non-standard applications

> **Case study**
>
> Cameron grew up and studied in Perth, Western Australia. He is currently studying for his SQE in order to be admitted as a solicitor in England and Wales.
>
> 'Out of high school, I wasn't clear on the career I wanted to pursue, and was drawn to the various legal and non-legal options that a law degree can offer. I was also drawn to learning about writing and drafting, government and politics and how businesses operate generally.
>
> 'Out of university, I was interested more in the commercial side of things, and worked in logistics and procurement. It took some time before I decided to pursue a career in law, and to complete practical legal studies in order to be admitted as a solicitor in Western Australia. A few years ago, I moved from Australia to the UK, and have been working as an in-house legal advisor since arriving. I am now studying for the SQE in order to be able to practise in England and Wales.
>
> 'My current role involves working closely with business stakeholders to negotiate client and supplier contracts, as well as reviewing and implementing internal policies and procedures to ensure regulatory and procedural compliance. In addition, my role also involves protecting the business from risk.
>
> 'To be successful in law, it is really important to identify the areas that you find most interesting. Getting involved is the best way of moving forward in that field as gaining hands-on experience will allow you to develop your knowledge of the area and to gain practical skills at the same time.'

10 | Open-and-shut case: Results day

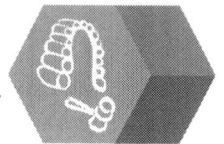

A level results day is arguably one of the most important days of your life, but don't panic: this chapter will provide you with some calm and practical advice on what to do on the day, whatever your results are.

The A level results will arrive at your school on the third Thursday in August. The universities will have received them a few days earlier. It is much better for you to go into school in person on the day the results are published, so do not arrange to be away on holiday then. Do not wait for the results to be emailed to you. Try to get hold of your results as soon as possible on the day – if you need to act to secure your place or go through Clearing, then time is of the essence as you will be competing with other students in the same situation.

If you live overseas and are unable to go into school, make sure that you get hold of your results in some other way as soon as possible on results day.

Hopefully, you will need to do nothing other than celebrate! If you have a conditional offer and your grades equal or exceed that offer, then you can relax and wait for your chosen university to send you joining instructions. To check that all is in order, you can log on to the 'Track' facility on the UCAS website to make sure that your place has been confirmed.

> **Caution!**
>
> You cannot assume that equivalent grades such as A*AB will satisfy an AAA offer. Always check with your chosen university.

If your results are not as good as you had expected, or better than you expected, or you did not receive an offer from any of your chosen universities, then there are a number of options.

What to do if your grades are significantly better than anticipated

You may have significantly beaten the terms of your firm offer and now think that you might like to go somewhere 'better'. Students who might have been predicted low grades and therefore applied to universities that would accept them rather than those where they would really like to study, can contact universities directly or try for different courses through Clearing.

Alternatively, you may choose to withdraw from UCAS and reapply the following year with your higher grades. This is a gamble, and you will need to determine the level of risk.

What to do if you hold an offer but miss the grades

If you have only narrowly missed the required grades (either for your 'firm' or 'insurance' choice), it is important that you contact the university as soon as possible on results day, because you may be able to persuade the university to consider you.

If you miss the grades for your firm choice, but meet the grades for your insurance choice, you will be able to accept the insurance place. However, you can still contact your first-choice institution, or an alternative, preferred institution, to see whether or not they are able to accept you (if they are, you will still have to enter into Clearing to accept it). A lot changes on results day, and those that are offered places may decline or defer them, meaning that though the likelihood of receiving your first-choice place is slim, it is worth a try. If unsuccessful, you also have the option to release yourself into Clearing on results day via your UCAS Hub if you decide you don't want to take up your insurance place.

If you do not achieve the grades required for either your firm or insurance choice, and you are unable to persuade either university still to accept you, then you are eligible to enter Clearing. This is a list of places that are still available on various courses at all of the universities. The list is published on the UCAS website. Places on law degrees available through Clearing will be few and far between, but if there is a place available at a university you would be interested in going to, then you must contact the university by telephone as quickly as possible on results day, because you will be competing with other students in the same position. Clearing is a stressful system, but it is important to contact universities that you would consider studying at in a logical and calm manner. You can acquire a number of verbal offers which will later appear on your UCAS page, which gives you some time to consider your options. You must make your decision carefully and in a measured way despite the time pressure. There is no point in accepting a place at a university where you do not realistically want to study.

In reality, due to the popularity of law as a degree, you should not pin your hopes on obtaining an offer of a place through Clearing. You may find that despite your best efforts, there simply are not any places available on law courses at universities where you would want to study. If you are unable to obtain a suitable place through Clearing, your best option would be to withdraw from UCAS altogether and then wait and reapply in the next academic year to courses for which you meet the entry requirements, with the benefit of your A level results to support your application. Given what has been said about the importance of choosing your university law course in Chapter 6, you do not want to settle for any university just because it has a place available, but hold out for a place at a university you are actually really enthusiastic about attending. In the meantime, you can use the time constructively by getting some work experience to build up your CV. You may also want to consider retaking some or all of your A levels in order to improve your chances of getting into a university you are really interested in going to.

What to do if you have no offer

If you did not receive any offers, you may have managed to find an offer through UCAS Extra. This scheme allows you to apply to other universities, either for law or for other courses. You will automatically be sent details by UCAS. UCAS Extra starts at the end of February and usually ends in July. If UCAS Extra does not provide you with an offer, you can enter Clearing in August once you have your results.

However, if you did not receive any offers when you applied, perhaps because your predicted results were not particularly strong, but you have ended up with better A level results than expected, then you need to make universities aware of this. Try to get in touch with them as early as possible on results day to see if they will reconsider their decision in the light of your results. The best way to do this is by telephone and email, and your UCAS referee may be able to help you in this respect. Try to persuade your referee to ring the admissions officers on your behalf – they will find it easier to get through than you will – or to email universities a note in support of your application; while many universities will not talk to your referee on your behalf on the day, this support can be recognised by universities in some circumstances.

Retaking your A levels

This may be a sensible option for students who know they are capable of achieving better grades than they did first time round. However, you should be aware that the grade requirements for retake candidates are often higher than for first-timers. You should investigate the particular universities you are interested in to find out what they require from retake students, as this due diligence will undoubtedly pay off. While there are some universities that rarely consider retake applications (except in the case of mitigating circumstances), many universities welcome applications from students who are so driven to study at their university that they are retaking their A levels to do so.

Extenuating circumstances

If your grades were below those that were predicted or expected because of extenuating circumstances, such as illness or family problems during exam time, make sure that you have written confirmation of this (such as a letter from a doctor, solicitor or someone at your school or college) and send this to the admissions department for your chosen course, as well as asking the exams officer at your school to pass this information on to the examining boards. The extenuating circumstances should be serious enough to merit special consideration and not just minor irritations.

Ideally, if something does go wrong at the time you are sitting your exams, you or your school/college should inform the universities immediately, warning them that you might not achieve the grades. It is more likely that they can make concessions then rather than when they have already made decisions about who to accept when the results are issued. For extenuating circumstances to be considered, universities often expect evidence to have been submitted to the relevant exam board for the affected exam.

If you are retaking your A levels or reapplying to university because of extenuating circumstances, it is good practice to email the admissions department outlining your academic profile and the circumstances that prevented you from securing the grades that you required, asking them whether they would be happy to consider your application. Generally, universities are transparent with their answer, and this is extremely useful when selecting which universities to put down on your UCAS form.

> **Case study**
>
> Initially, Jade was unsure about what to pursue as a career. She ultimately decided that law would be the best fit after completing an extremely worthwhile work experience placement.
>
> 'I chose to study law once I realised I wanted to become a solicitor, which was confirmed after my work experience in a law firm. I also knew that law was a degree that a number of different avenues could flow from due to the many different transferable skills it teaches, and this was appealing to me.
>
> 'At A level I studied Biology, Chemistry and Religious Studies. I originally applied to do dentistry, which I missed out on the grades for. During my year of resits, I decided I no longer wanted to do dentistry and instead applied to do psychology. After one semester, I quickly realised that psychology was not the right fit for me

and I decided to look to law as it had always been a field I'd been interested in but had never pursued.

'I undertook three weeks' work experience at a local law firm who specialised in criminal, property and family law. I was able to attend the Magistrates' Court alongside a criminal lawyer and watch a number of various cases, mostly involving driving offences, which allowed me a brief insight into the court system. In addition, I was able to read criminal case files and I had the opportunity to discuss these cases with senior solicitors, which was really interesting and enabled me to see the ethical dilemmas some criminal lawyers face and how they deal with it. The majority of the work I carried out at the law firm was in the conveyancing department, and I was fortunate enough to be offered a job as a legal assistant in this department prior to starting my degree. During this time, I gained a lot of experience writing letters to clients and emails to other solicitor's firms, as well as answering client phone calls. I also learnt how to draft contracts involving the sale and purchases of property, as well as organising files for property transactions. My work experience really gave me an insight into the workings of a local law firm and how the life of a solicitor plays out in reality. The experience I had here assured me that law was definitely what I wanted to study.

'Overall, my experience of studying law so far has been a positive one. My first year was during the pandemic, which meant that all learning was online. This was quite daunting as the only interaction I had with my peers and the law school faculty was through Zoom. However, being back on campus for second year is great. Studying law involves a lot of reading, a common preconception that is actually true. Once you get to grips for what you are looking for within a case and key concepts, this becomes much easier. At first, I found that I was spending hours combing through information but with practice this has become something I find interesting and actually enjoy.

'The modules studied are fairly diverse, and alongside studying the better-known modules of criminal law, land law, etc., we study modules such as Law in Action and Decolonising Legal Concepts; these give us free rein to research a topic and are thought provoking. Our week is composed of about 10 hours of lectures plus seminars; lectures allow us to have a briefer explanation of legal concepts, whereas seminars are where an in-depth discussion of these topics occurs and where you get a chance to speak with peers and your seminar leader so that a better understanding forms. The exams and assignments so far have been essay- or problem question-based. Problem questions have become my favourite form of exam – you are given scenarios and get the opportunity to put on a "lawyer hat" and advise the parties in the scenario by applying the concepts we have learnt in that particular module.

'The heavy workload is something that was first hard to get to grips with, and you will end up spending most of your time independently studying. It is the work that is done outside of lectures that counts, which includes preparing for seminars, reading cases, working through assignments. This is manageable, but it can take a number of weeks to get used to a routine and structure.

'Making sure you are organised is a big tip for anyone studying law, as with a routine you can still get everything done and have down time as well. I usually study from 9am–5pm, and then I have the rest of the day to enjoy university life. Getting involved with extra-curricular activities is also important, universities often have pro-bono groups or law societies you can join, and this is really important when it comes to applying for vacation schemes. It is good to start interacting early with any extracurricular activities your law school may offer. A good aspect of the course at my university is a scheme run for students that provides talks around future plans post-graduation. Actually doing the reading that is set, whether that be legal journal articles, cases, textbooks, etc., is critical, because this is what amplifies your knowledge and enables higher grades. Maybe before starting Law School read a case or a legal journal to get a feel of the type of thing you'll be expected to read. Keeping up to date with happenings in the legal field will also help to build up legal awareness, and I recommend *Legal Cheek* as a good, easy read for potential law students.

'An important thing for me when picking a course was that I wanted to be learning something I not only found interesting but would also be able to use in future life. This is something I really feel you get from studying law. In 10 years' time, I hope to be a solicitor working in commercial law.'

Students with disabilities and special educational needs

For the most part, universities are able to accommodate students with a wide range of disabilities and special educational needs. As such, they are encouraged to apply to study law. On the UCAS form, there is a section that allows students to disclose such information, and it is recommended that a full description of the disabilities or special educational needs be provided, as well as the support required. All institutions are committed to supporting students with such considerations, but it is always worth contacting each institution and, where possible, the specific department, to determine how much support they will be able to offer. Most institutions will have a dedicated team of equality and diversity advisors employed solely to provide guidance and support.

When you receive an offer from a university, they should follow up with you directly regarding the disabilities outlined on your UCAS form. It is vital that you ensure there is complete transparency at this stage, as a lack of coherence or failure to reveal a full picture may result in complications in securing appropriate accommodation and could even result in withdrawal from the course.

It is also worth considering how accessible a career in law is for someone with a disability. The Equality Act (2010) has ensured that workplaces put the appropriate measures in place, as much as possible, to allow disabled people to thrive in the workplace. In theory, there is no barrier to working as a lawyer with a physical disability, though it is evident that not all workplaces will be suitable. Large solicitors' firms, for example, are likely to comprise appropriate disability measures such as lifts and adapted entrances and exits, whereas smaller firms may not have the means to adjust.

Students with special educational needs who require support in the form of additional time in exams, for example, will need to provide the appropriate supporting documentation. As long as this can be provided, there should be no issues in securing these arrangements.

The Central Criminal Court of England and Wales is commonly known by what name?

Answer: The Old Bailey

11 | Bail out: Fees and funding

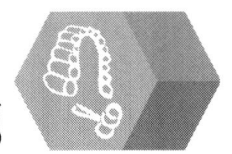

Seeking to qualify as a lawyer is expensive: first you have to fund a university degree and then you need to fund the SQE (possibly preceded by a postgraduate qualification in law, such as the GDL in England and Wales, if your degree was not in law). This chapter looks at the fees for the university degree stage of qualification and how those fees are funded, and the fees and funding arrangements for postgraduate studies in law and the vocational stages of training (see also Chapter 4). This chapter briefly outlines the current fee structure for UK universities and the way in which the governments of the constituent countries of the UK help students fund their university studies. More information can be found at www.gov.uk/student-finance.

UK students

The tuition fee that you will have to pay for undergraduate courses will depend on where you live and where you intend to study. Universities are allowed to charge home undergraduate fees up to £9,250 per year, as part of the government's Teaching Excellence Framework (TEF), which assesses universities and colleges on the quality of their teaching. The fee cap for students studying in Wales remains at £9,000, while fees for students in Northern Ireland are a maximum of £9,250 for 2024 entry. These fees have been the same for a number of years and have been frozen until at least the 2024/2025 academic year, but increases are expected in the future.

There are a number of variations between the systems in England, Scotland, Wales and Northern Ireland, which can result in significant differences between the fees that are ultimately paid by students. Currently (for 2023/2024 entry) the rules are as follows, although they may be subject to change in the future.

- Students from England are required to pay a maximum of £9,250 if they are studying in England, Scotland or Northern Ireland, and up to £9,000 if they are studying in Wales.
- Students from Wales pay up to £9,000 if they study in Wales, or up to £9,250 if they study in England, Scotland or Northern Ireland.
- Students from Scotland who study at Scottish universities are not required to pay tuition fees (or, rather, tuition fees of £1,820 for

2024 entry are covered the Student Awards Agency for Scotland (SAAS) for students who qualify for home student status). Scottish students have to pay fees of up to £9,250 if they study in England or Northern Ireland, and up to £9,000 if they study in Wales.
- Students living in Northern Ireland pay up to £4,710 if they attend university in Northern Ireland, up to £9,250 if they study in England or Scotland, and up to £9,000 if they study in Wales.

EU students

At present, EU students are charged the same fees as charged to non-EU international students, which are significantly higher than those charged to UK students and are determined by each university. Some students from the EU may be eligible for some support in terms of student loans from the UK government, but this is dependent on a number of factors, so it is best to check personal eligibility. Students from the Republic of Ireland are exempt from paying higher fees and are eligible for home fee status.

Living expenses

Your living expenses include the cost of your accommodation, food, clothes, travel and equipment, leisure and social activities – plus possible extras like field trips and study visits, if these aren't covered by the tuition fees.

Check university and college websites for information about possible living costs. Some offer more detailed advice than others and give breakdowns under various headings such as accommodation, food and daily travel. Others go even further and give typical weekly, monthly or annual spends.

If you're living away from home, accommodation will make up the largest proportion of your living costs. There is likely to be a range of accommodation options – from a standard room in university halls through to privately rented accommodation – with a range of price points. You'll probably be surprised when you do some research to find that the cheapest and most expensive towns are not as you might have expected; the cost of accommodation often depends on how much of it is available in a particular area.

When choosing accommodation, it is essential to consider its location and factor in the cost of travel to your university or college. It is also important to find out what's included in the accommodation costs (such as utilities, personal property insurance and Wi-Fi) and whether it is possible to pay for accommodation during term time only.

Funding your studies

How do you fund your time in higher education? Don't ignore this question and leave it until the last minute! You will need to think carefully about how to budget for several years' costs – and you need to know what help you might get from:

- the government
- your family or partner
- paid part-time work
- other sources, such as bursaries and scholarships.

This chapter gives a brief overview of a complicated funding situation, which can vary according to where you come from and where you plan to study. For more details about the different types of funding available and how to apply for them, check your regional student finance website:

- www.gov.uk/contact-student-finance-england
- www.saas.gov.uk
- www.studentfinanceni.co.uk
- www.studentfinancewales.co.uk

Tuition fee loans

For UK students, tuition fees can be covered by taking out a tuition fee loan, which will be paid directly to your university or college at the start of each year of your course. You are effectively given a loan by the government that you repay through your income tax from the April after you finish your course but only once your earnings reach a certain threshold. Currently, these income thresholds stand at:

- £25,000 per year for students from England
- £27,295 a year for students from Wales
- £27,660 for students from Scotland (who go to university outside of Scotland)
- £22,015 for students from Northern Ireland

(All figures apply to students starting their course after 1 August 2023.)

So, if you never reach this threshold, you will not have to repay the fees. In addition, any outstanding balance on your loan will be cancelled after a certain period of time if you have not already cleared it in full. The length of time depends on the rules at the time you took out the loan. For students in England who started their studies in September 2023, the repayment period was extended to 40 years (from 30 years), so it is recommended that students in other regions keep a close eye on any developments with respect to the length of the loan repayment period.

The current situation regarding repayments is that you repay 9% of anything you earn over the annual income threshold.

The interest rate charged on student loans depends on what repayment plan you are on, but for students in England who started their course after 1 August 2023 (Plan 5) it is set at the RPI (Retail Price Index) rate of inflation.

Maintenance loans

In addition to a tuition fee loan, all students can apply for a maintenance or living cost loan. All students are entitled to a maintenance loan; however, the amount you can borrow will be dependent on your household income – in other words, it is means tested. 'Household income' refers to your family's gross annual income (their income before tax). With the exception of loans available to Scottish students, the amount you can claim also varies depending on your living situation, with the maximum loan being available to students living away from home in London.

Each regional student finance website includes a finance calculator tool that will give an estimate of the finance you would be eligible for based on your family income and other factors, and it is well worth looking at this before planning your budget.

England (2024/2025)

The maximum annual maintenance loan in England:

- £8,610 for those living in the family home
- £10,227 for those living away from home (£13,348 in London).

Wales (2023/2024)

In Wales, students can get a combination of a maintenance grant, which they do not have to pay back, and a maintenance loan. Although the grants are means tested, most students will get a grant of at least £1,000.

The maximum amounts for maintenance loans and grants in Wales:

- £9,950 for those living in the family home
- £11,720 for those living away from home (£14,635 in London).

Scotland (2024/2025)

In Scotland, students can get a mix of maintenance loans and non-repayable bursaries (grants) to cover living expenses. These are as follows (all figures per year):

- household income up to £20,999: £2,000 bursary and £9,400 loan
- household income £21,000–£23,999: £1,125 bursary and £9,400 loan
- household income £24,000–£33,999: £500 bursary and £9,400 loan
- household income £34,000 and above: no bursary and £8,400 loan.

Unlike the rest of the UK, household income for Scottish students is measured on the income bands listed on page 158 rather than exact household income.

Northern Ireland (2023/24)

The maximum annual maintenance loan in Northern Ireland:

- £5,250 for those living in the family home
- £6,776 for those living away from home (£9,492 in London).

In addition, you may be eligible for a non-repayable maintenance grant if your household income is below £41,065 and it is paid to you. This is paid alongside any maintenance loan you qualify for and is up to £3,475.

Bursaries and scholarships

UK universities now offer a wide range of bursaries and scholarships to support some of their students. In order to charge the maximum permitted tuition fees of £9,250, universities must prove that they are awarding bursaries to poorer students. These are contributions towards the cost of going to university that do not have to be repaid. The terms of these will vary between the universities and you should check the universities' websites carefully to see whether you may be able to apply for any financial help. Usually, bursaries are completely dependent on your household income, whereas scholarships are at least partly dependent on academic or extra-curricular (e.g. sporting) ability.

The Law Society details a number of opportunities available for funding your studies, which can be accessed via their website (www.lawsociety.org.uk/career-advice/becoming-a-solicitor/funding-and-support-during-your-studies-internships-scholarships-and-sponsors).

Funding the SQE

From 2021, the SQE was introduced as a new pathway of qualifying to become a solicitor. SQE1 costs £1,622 and SQE2 costs £2,493 (totalling £4,115). At present, there are no funding options for the SQE itself or for standalone SQE preparation courses, though the Law Society is working to establish a source of funding for those who need it.

Funding the GDL, LPC and BPTC

Though the qualification route for solicitors and barristers in England and Wales is changing, here are existing funding options available for these pathways, which are set out overleaf.

GDL

The GDL is an expensive but unavoidable way of qualifying as a lawyer for graduates without QLDs before the complete introduction of the SQE. Unfortunately, postgraduate funding is not an option for covering GDL fees, but there are a number of ways of obtaining financial support. Often, GDL students will need to combine a number of sources of funding to pay the fees and support themselves for the duration. Some providers recognise the cost implications and now offer part-time courses and instalment payment plans, so research the stance of the provider on this when applying.

Perhaps the most obvious way to secure funding is to determine whether the GDL provider offers any scholarships or bursaries. You need to be on the ball with these, as they tend to be competitive with early deadlines. Many law firms will offer to cover the fees of the GDL if a training contract is secured early, with some even providing a maintenance grant to support with living costs. Some will even pay retrospectively if a training contract is secured mid-GDL, but the stance of law firms doing so is highly variable, so research carefully and check with them directly. The Law Society also offers a bursary scheme and these are awarded on the applicant's merit.

Graduate loans are also available through high street banks. These are not always ideal as repayments often start immediately, so be sure to exhaust all other options first.

LPC

As with the GDL, the LPC is a costly but crucial element of qualifying as a solicitor. Many of the funding options are the same as with the GDL, with the option of part-time study being popular as it allows students to work part-time, too. Scholarships and bursaries will be available from course providers and the Law Society, including the DAS scheme (as outlined in Chapter 4), and law firms will often fund your training once you have secured a training contract.

Though Student Finance Postgraduate Loans do not cover a standard LPC, the University of Law has now started offering master's degrees in law with integrated LPCs, thereby qualifying the training for this source of funding. This will mean that your fees are covered, and you will complete both the LPC and a master's degree simultaneously, so it is certainly worth consideration!

BPTC

Scholarships for the BPTC can be accessed through the Inns of Court, and these are the most significant sources of funding for this particular stage of training. Some chambers offer pupillage awards if a pupillage is secured prior to the commencement of the BPTC, but this is quite rare.

The BPTC can also be funded using a Professional Career and Development Loan, though it is recommended that all scholarship options be researched first.

> *Did you know?*
>
> *It is illegal to stand within 100 yards of the reigning monarch without wearing socks.*

12 | All rights reserved: Further information

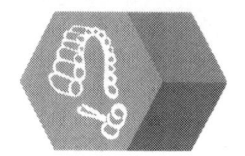

Useful websites

Legal professions

Solicitors
- The Law Society (of England and Wales): www.lawsociety.org.uk; www.lawsociety.org.uk/en/topics/research/annual-statistics-report-2022
- The Law Society of Northern Ireland: www.lawsoc-ni.org
- The Law Society of Scotland: www.lawscot.org.uk
- Solicitors Regulation Authority: www.sra.org.uk

Barristers
- The Bar Council of England and Wales: www.barcouncil.org.uk
- The Bar Standards Board: www.barstandardsboard.org.uk; www.barstandardsboard.org.uk/news-publications/research-and-statistics/statistics-about-the-bar.html
- The Faculty of Advocates in Scotland: www.advocates.org.uk
- Gray's Inn: www.graysinn.org.uk
- The Inner Temple: www.innertemple.org.uk
- Lincoln's Inn: www.lincolnsinn.org.uk
- The Middle Temple: www.middletemple.org.uk
- Northern Ireland Bar: www.barofni.com

Other legal professions
- Law costs draftsmen: www.associationofcostslawyers.co.uk
- Legal executives: www.cilex.org.uk
- Legal secretaries: www.institutelegalsecretaries.com
- Licensed conveyancers: www.clc-uk.org
- Notaries: www.thenotariessociety.org.uk
- Paralegals: www.theiop.org
- Patent attorneys: www.cipa.org.uk
- Trademark attorneys: www.citma.org.uk/home

12 Further information

Legal profession: directories

- Chambers UK and Chambers UK Bar Guide: https://chambers.com; Chambers publishes comprehensive online directories, containing ranking tables and commentary, of firms of solicitors and barristers' chambers. They are also published annually in print format.
- Legal 500: www.legal500.com; an in-depth survey of the UK legal profession, also published annually in print format.
- TARGETjobs: https://targetjobs.co.uk/careers-products; TARGETjobs publishes online graduate careers guides and directories for various professions including law:
  – TARGETjobs: Law
  – TARGETjobs: Law vacation schemes & Mini pupillages
  – TARGETjobs: Law Pupillages Handbook.
- Law firm gossip: www.rollonfriday.com

Legal systems

- Ministry of Justice: www.justice.gov.uk
- Northern Ireland:
  www.niassembly.gov.uk
  www.gov.uk/guidance/devolution-settlement-northern-ireland
  www.nidirect.gov.uk/information-and-services/crime-justice-and-law
- Scotland: www.scotcourts.gov.uk/about-the-scottish-court-service
- Wales: www.assemblywales.org

Other legal organisations

- Crown Prosecution Service: www.cps.gov.uk
- Legal Action Group: www.lag.org.uk

Education and training

A levels
- Access to Higher Education courses: www.accesstohe.ac.uk
- Russell Group: www.russellgroup.ac.uk
- UK qualification providers overseas: https://study-uk.britishcouncil.org

University applications
- LNAT: www.lnat.ac.uk
- UCAS: www.ucas.com
- UCAS Parent Guide (information about the UCAS undergraduate application process): www.ucas.com/undergraduate/applying-university/ucas-undergraduate-advice-parents-and-guardians
- UCAS reference: www.ucas.com/advisers/writing-references/changes-undergraduate-references-2024-entry

- University guides:
    www.thecompleteuniversityguide.co.uk
    www.theguardian.com/education/ng-interactive/2022/sep/24/the-guardian-university-guide-2023-the-rankings
- University of Cambridge law: www.law.cam.ac.uk
- University open days: www.opendays.com

Law interviews
- Cambridge: www.undergraduate.study.cam.ac.uk/apply/after/cambridge-interviews
- Oxford:
    www.ox.ac.uk/admissions/undergraduate/applying-to-oxford/guide/interviews/interview-timetable
    www.ox.ac.uk/admissions/undergraduate/applying-to-oxford/guide/interviews
- York: www.york.ac.uk/study/undergraduate/appplying

Fees and funding
- England: www.gov.uk/student-finance
- Northern Ireland: www.studentfinanceni.co.uk
- Overseas students: www.ukcisa.org.uk
- Scotland: www.saas.gov.uk
- Wales: www.studentfinancewales.co.uk

Vocational training
- Bar Course Aptitude Test (BCAT): www.barstandardsboard.org.uk/training-qualification/bar-qualification-manual/part-2-for-students-pupils--transferring-lawyers/b3-the-bar-course-aptitude-test-bcat.html
- Bar Standards Board (Becoming a barrister): www.barstandardsboard.org.uk/training-qualification/becoming-a-barrister.html
- Central Applications Board (for GDL and LPC): www.lawcabs.ac.uk
- GDL course providers: www.sra.org.uk/become-solicitor/legal-practice-course-route/qualifying-law-degree-common-professional-examination/cpe-gdl-course-providers/
- Pupillage Gateway: www.pupillagegateway.com

SQE
- Law Society – Solicitors Qualifying Exam (SQE): www.lawsociety.org.uk/career-advice/becoming-a-solicitor/solicitors-qualifying-examination-sqe
- Solicitors' Regulation Authority – Solicitors Qualifying Examination (SQE) route: www.sra.org.uk/become-solicitor/sqe

Funding training
- Diversity Access Scheme: www.lawsociety.org.uk/campaigns/diversity-access-scheme
- Postgraduate loans: www.gov.uk/postgraduate-loan

- Sponsorship: TARGET jobs: https://targetjobs.co.uk/careers-advice/law/which-law-firms-will-fund-your-lpc-and-gdl-course-fees-and-pay

Careers

- www.lawcareers.net
- www.simplylawjobs.com

Law reports

- www.bailii.org

Useful books

University entrance

Getting into Oxford & Cambridge 2025 Entry, Trotman, 2024.
HEAP 2025: University Degree Course Offers, Brian Heap, Trotman, 2024.
How to Complete Your UCAS Application 2025 Entry, Ryan Moran & UCAS, Trotman, 2024.
How to Write a Winning Personal Statement, Ian Stannard, Trotman Education, 2016.
The Times Good University Guide 2024, Times Books, 2024.
The University Choice Journal, Barbara Bassot, Trotman Education, 2017.
University Interviews, Ian Stannard and Godfrey Cooper, Trotman Education, 2017.

LNAT

Mastering the National Admissions Test for Law, M Shepherd, Routledge, 2013.
Passing the LNAT, R Hutton and G Hutton, Learning Matters, 2011.

Studying law

Glanville Williams: Learning the Law, A T H Smith, Sweet & Maxwell, 2010. (This book, first published in 1945, is a very popular introductory book containing lots of useful information on studying law.)
Is Eating People Wrong? Great Legal Cases and How They Shaped the World, A Hutchinson, Cambridge University Press, 2010.
Learning Legal Rules: A Students' Guide to Legal Method and Reasoning, 8th edition, J A Holland and J S Webb, OUP, 2013.
Letters to a Law Student: A Guide to Studying Law at University, Nicholas J McBride, Pearson, 2013.
What about Law? Studying Law at University, 2nd edition, C Barnard, J O'Sullivan and G J Virgo, Hart Publishing, 2011.

The English legal system

The Discipline of Law, Lord Denning, OUP, 2005.
The English Legal System, Jacqueline Martin, Hodder Education, 2013.
Introduction to the English Legal System 2019-2020, M Partington, OUP, 2019.
The Law Machine, Marcel Berlins and Clare Dyer, Penguin, 2000.
The Law (Theory and Practice in British Politics), J Waldron, Routledge, 1990.
Legal Method, Palgrave Macmillan Law Masters, 2013.
Politics of the Judiciary, J A G Griffith, Fontana, 2010.

The criminal justice system and miscarriages of justice

Blind Justice: Miscarriages of Justice in Twentieth Century Britain, John Eddleston, ABC-CLIO, 2000.
The Juryman's Tale, T Grove, Bloomsbury, 2000.
The Magistrate's Tale, T Grove, Bloomsbury, 2003.
A Matter of Justice, M Zander, OUP, 1989.
Memoirs of a Radical Lawyer, Michael Mansfield, Bloomsbury, 2010.
Miscarriages of Justice: A Review of 'Justice in Error', C Walker and K Starmer (eds), OUP, 1999.
Standing Accused, M McConville et al, OUP, 1994.

Careers

Is Law for You?: Deciding If You Want to Study Law, Christopher Stoakes, Christopher Stoakes Ltd, 2013.
Tomorrow's Lawyers: An Introduction to Your Future, Richard Susskind, OUP, 2013.

Professional journals

The Law Society Gazette
www.lawgazette.co.uk
(Publication for solicitors in England and Wales.)

The Lawyer
www.thelawyer.com
(Website for the legal professions containing news, analysis and comment.)

Legal Action
www.lag.org.uk/magazine
(Monthly magazine of the Legal Action Group, the access to justice charity.)

Legal Business
www.legalbusiness.co.uk
(Monthly magazine for legal professionals.)

Glossary

Administrative law
Law governing the duties and operations of the government and public authorities. A branch of public law, usually studied with constitutional law. One of the core subjects.

Advocate
A person who represents someone in court, arguing the case on their behalf. Barristers are the traditional advocates in the English legal system, but solicitors can also now conduct advocacy in certain cases. Advocates in Scotland are the equivalent of English barristers.

Bar
Collective term for the barristers' profession. Aspiring barristers are 'called to the Bar'. The Bar Council is the representative body for barristers.

Bar Professional Training Course (BPTC)
Vocational training course (of one year if studied full-time) for future barristers, taken after completing a law degree (or non-law degree followed by the Graduate Diploma in Law).

Black-letter law
A well-established law that is no longer in dispute.

Brexit
The withdrawal of the UK from the European Union on 31 January 2020.

Chambers
Offices occupied by a group of barristers. The term also describes a group of barristers practising from a set of chambers.

Civil law
Can mean either:
- private law, as opposed to criminal, administrative, military and church law; or
- the system of law that grew from Roman law as opposed to the English system of common law.

Common law
Law derived from case law: that is, law created by judges and developed on a case-by-case basis, rather than laws enacted by Parliament.

Constitutional law
The rules and practices determining how the state is governed, defining the functions of the different entities within a state – i.e. the executive

(government), the legislature (Parliament) and the judiciary, and regulating the relationship between the individual and the state. The constitution of the UK remains largely unwritten, unlike most other states. It is usually studied with administrative law and is one of the core subjects.

Contract law (law of contract)
The law governing contracts, i.e. legally binding agreements (written, verbal or even implied) between two or more parties. Contracts arise as a result of offer and acceptance, although there are several other criteria that must be satisfied for an agreement to be legally binding. One of the core subjects.

Core subjects
The foundation subjects that must be studied during a degree if the degree is a Qualifying Law Degree, which satisfies the academic stage of training requirements to qualify as a lawyer. Currently these are constitutional and administrative law; contract law; tort; criminal law; equity and trusts; European Union law and property/land law.

Criminal law
The law defining those acts that are deemed to be public wrongs and are therefore punishable by the state in criminal proceedings. Most crimes are made up of two elements – the act itself (*actus reus*) and the thinking behind it (*mens rea*), both of which must be proved 'beyond reasonable doubt' in court to establish guilt. Criminal law is one of the core subjects.

Crown Prosecution Service (CPS)
The CPS, headed by the Director of Public Prosecutions (DPP), is responsible for virtually all the criminal proceedings brought by the police in England and Wales.

Delict (law of delict)
The Scottish name for tort.

Equity
The part of English law originally developed by the Lord Chancellor (and later by the Court of Chancery) to do justice where the common law remedies were limited in scope and flexibility and would lead to an unfair result: equity was more concerned with a fair result than the rigid principles of the law. Even now, equity prevails over the rules of law, but the system of equity is no longer as arbitrary as before. The main areas of equity now cover trusts, property and remedies (e.g. injunctions). 'Anton Piller' orders are a more recent example of equity at work. Equity is studied with trusts as one of the core subjects.

European Union law
The laws of the European Union and how they impact on the English legal system. One of the core subjects.

Glossary

Evidence
Something that proves the existence or non-existence of a fact. The law of evidence refers to the rules governing the presentation of facts and proof in court, including whether or not evidence is admissible.

Graduate Diploma in Law (GDL)
Also known as the Common Professional Examination (CPE). The one-year (full-time) course that non-law graduates can take to satisfy the academic stage of training to become a lawyer. It covers the seven core subjects that would be studied in a qualifying law degree.

Jurisprudence
The philosophy and theories of law.

Jury
Group of (usually 12) people who are selected at random to give a verdict in court.

Land law (property law)
The law of rights in different types of property and how these rights may be established or transferred. It covers subjects such as mortgages, property trusts, landlord and tenant, leases, easements and covenants. One of the core subjects.

Law school
A law department within a university.

Legal Practice Course (LPC)
The vocational one-year (full-time) training course taken after graduation with a qualifying degree, or after taking the GDL, and prior to the two-year training contract, designed for intending solicitors.

Moot
A mock courtroom trial of a hypothetical case organised as an extra-curricular/optional activity to help develop legal skills of presenting a clear, logical argument and questioning a witness.

Obligations (law of obligations)
Another name for the laws of tort and contract.

Private law
The parts of the law that deal with the relationships between individuals that are of no direct concern to the state. It includes property law, trusts, contract, tort and family law.

Property law
See land law.

Public law
Law dealing with the constitution and functions of the organs of government, the relationship between individuals and the state and the relationships between individuals that are of direct concern to the state. It includes constitutional law, administrative law, tax law and criminal law.

Pupillage
The final stage of training to become a barrister, involving shadowing a qualified barrister for two six-month periods.

Solicitors Qualifying Examination (SQE)
A series of assessments set by Kaplan that must be passed by all aspiring solicitors after 2021 in order to qualify. This will ultimately replace GDLs and the LPC.

Statute
A law passed by Parliament.

Statute book
All statutes that are currently in force.

Tort
A wrongful act or omission for which the person who has been wronged can obtain damages (i.e. compensation) in a civil court. The definition does not include breaches of contract. Most torts involve personal injury or damage to property caused by negligence. Other torts are defamation, nuisance, etc. The law of tort is one of the core subjects.

Training contract
The two-year period of on-the-job training undertaken by all future solicitors after the LPC in order to complete the vocational stage of training.

Trusts
A legal arrangement whereby one or more trustees hold property for the benefit of one or more beneficiaries. The property is said to be held 'on trust'. Studied with equity as one of the core subjects.